I AM NOT A CHILD MOLESTER

I AM NOT A CHILD MOLESTER

T.J. KEREKES, III

Library of Congress Control Number: 2025907511

ISBN: 979-8-89228-552-0 (Paperback)
ISBN: 979-8-89228-553-7 (eBook)

Printed in the United States of America

To my mom and my dad and my kids and family and friends like Tony & Brenda and the Bergs, Bullocks, Chachras, Adens, coaches Hussey & McCarthy and so many more dear people too many to mention here that helped us along the way, but mostly for my mom……

TABLE OF CONTENTS

PROLOGUE

With all the news this past decade about women in the 'Me Too' movement coming forward to reveal violations perpetrated upon them years ago most often by men, what about me when a young girl misled me about her age which led to me getting arrested and convicted and yet I NEVER EVEN KNEW I WAS BREAKING THE LAW! So I ask you what about me?

And please before you accuse me of belittling the 'Me Too' movement hear me out. That is not what I am trying to do at all. I am merely saying that, just as with the 'Me Too' movement, an event that occurred many years ago changed my life forever. But where these 'Me Too' women have felt liberated by coming forward, there is no liberation for me because I was branded with a felony conviction -- for life.

So I ask you what about me? How do you think it feels to be the pariah of any neighborhood anywhere you live; anywhere you live you are always the child molester who lives down the street. How do you think it feels to walk out the door every day and have to wonder who knows? How do you think it feels to have to avoid schools and children because you fear you might be accused of looking at someone the wrong way and you can't defend yourself because you are already guilty in their eyes.

How do you think it feels to see someone you know on the street and wonder are they going to speak or are they going to just pass you by as if they don't know you? And sometimes they do just pass you by and then you wonder did they not see you or do they know. How do you think it feels?

I lost jobs. I lost friends I liked and admired, friends like Steve and Ron and Ken - I liked them a lot - I want them to know the truth. I brought embarrassment to my family. I had to leave the small town I grew up in with my tail tucked between my legs because I couldn't find work. I have missed funerals of dear friends because I couldn't bear to face my old classmates and acquaintances. I never got the chance to defend myself those many years ago and now that I am growing old I want to tell my side before it is too late for me.

How do you think it feels having to lie every time you apply for a job because telling the truth means you don't stand a chance? How do you think it feels when you do finally get a job but then have to worry every day is this the day the shoe will drop? How do you think it feels? AND I NEVER EVEN KNEW I WAS BREAKING THE LAW.

Absolutely I made a mistake - I know I did. But to be branded for life for a crime I didn't even know I was committing was excessive. I was deceived. And why was I the only one held accountable? Where was the girl's mom? This girl and her cousin laid the plans that day; it was all a total surprise for me. Where was her accountability? Sadly she was only thirteen, but she was thirteen going on 30. She was tall for her age and wore a larger bra cup size than my wife whom I was separated with at the time did. To say this girl was mature for her age is an understatement, yet her physical appearance meant nothing to the state's prosecutor who had it out for me, had it out for me because he did not like that I was a nigger lover - my estranged wife and this young girl were both black. Forty years ago in the state of Virginia you just didn't do that, especially not in a small southwest Virginia town. The state prosecutor wanted to crush me and he succeeded -- for life.

For years I prayed the girl would come forward and tell the truth because the truth could possibly get me a new trial, but at this point in my life it doesn't matter anymore. All I want is to tell my side because I was denied that right years ago. For those who say there is no excuse because I was the adult and she was but a child, all I can say to them is that I took my medicine and I have paid my dues.

The bulk of this story was written 20 years ago and is just now being made public so some of the rhetoric may seem dated. I opted not to rewrite the entire manuscript because the facts from twenty years ago remain the same facts today. And sadly, many of the issues I comment on still exist today.

People have asked me why come forward now why bring attention to yourself after you have made it all this time you have survived the felony conviction why bring it up now at this point in your life and my answer is that I not only want to explain my actions because I never had the opportunity to before thanks to being treated as 'guilty before proven innocent', but also because if I can help bring attention to the fact that men can also be fooled by a member of the opposite sex too (no it is not an exclusively female thing) and help the next guy to avoid having to pay for the rest of his life then I have succeeded in my purpose.

My sentence was cruel and unusual punishment. No premeditation was involved, no intention to deceive on my part, no planning or conspiring, yet guilty for life as if I meant for it to all happen. I was/am a good person not some criminal. I had feelings for this girl that misled me and then suddenly overnight I was/am a monster to society. For Life.

My only hope is that society will take a closer look at all the circumstances before it is so quick to judge. The law is tough when it comes to this type of crime but it must allow both parties to state their case before passing judgement. I didn't get my chance.

I am not perfect but I am no monster. I happen to care about what people think of me; sometimes I wish I didn't but I do. Call it a character flaw. I have paid for my mistake every day of my life for 35 years now.

So this is my story. I want my good name back. I want my dignity back that was taken away from me. I am not afraid to come forward now because I have nothing to lose - there is nothing else society can do to me that it has not already done by branding me a child molester. But as God is my witness I AM NOT A CHILD MOLESTER.

The name of the young girl has been changed to protect the innocent.

CONVICTED…

In the year of 1991, I, a family man thirty-four years old with two young sons, was charged with and then convicted of Indecent Liberties with a minor, a Class IV felony, the lowest class of high crimes. With the conviction I was branded a child molester for life. Signed, sealed, sanctioned certified and delivered -- for life.

For my defense I waived my right to an attorney. Being of sound body and mind I felt I did not need a mouthpiece to defend the criminal charges against me. I was innocent and did not need, nor want, to hide behind some attorney. Nor did I wish to place my destiny in a stranger's hands. I was going to clear my name based on the facts and not clever legal technicalities, ploys, or payoffs.

And although I didn't put much stock in lawyers, I did have sufficient faith in the law. I believed in our legal system and its presumption of innocence until proven guilty. I believed that right does conquer wrong and that justice will prevail. I may as well have believed in the tooth fairy.

I never got an opportunity to defend myself in court. I never received that jury of my peers, the one guaranteed in the Constitution of the United States to each and every one of its citizens. I learned the hard way that I was mere shark bait in a system that had it out for me. I never stood a chance. I was doomed from the beginning, putty in the hands of a prejudiced judge and politically motivated prosecuting attorney who at the time was up for re-election. They did me wrong.

Looking back on it all I admit I made mistakes. I made a mistake getting involved with that young girl in the first place. I made a mistake not listening to advice from my family and friends after my arrest. My stubbornness would not let me listen to reason.

I made a mistake not taking the court appointed defense attorney, and I made a huge mistake not accepting my uncle's kind offer to cover all expenses for my legal defense.

But of all the mistakes I made, I feel my biggest one was giving up on hope and not standing up for my rights. I buckled from the pressure the system placed upon me. I wanted to hold out and be strong, I wanted to defend myself but my faith in our legal system simply vanished into thin air while sitting in a concrete jail cell. The possibility that I could be found guilty and sentenced to years in a prison suddenly overwhelmed me and I got scared - real scared. So scared that my faith in the truth didn't matter anymore, my belief in principals and integrity and righteousness simply dissolved and all I cared about was getting out of that box regardless of what it took. When you're sitting in a small concrete jail cell *everything* you know about your life simply vanishes into thin air.

In retrospect, waiving my right to an attorney was certainly not the brightest thing that I ever did. I didn't care much for lawyers then and I care even less for them today, but looking back I should have swallowed my pride and faced the fact that I was in big trouble and needed some professional help. But I was too stubborn to do the sensible thing.

You can call me stubborn, or hard headed, and I can't deny it. Call me gullible and I suppose I can't say no. Call me an idiot and I won't debate you on that either, but call me a child molester and I will emphatically deny it to the end because, as God is my witness, I am not a child molester and that is the truth...

...TRUTH

The truth is I was fooled. The young girl's name was April. I first met her after a sandlot football game one chilly autumn evening of 1990. My oldest son was played defensive end, much to my elation, as I was a big football fan. I was watching the game intently while at the same time cursing myself for not wearing a heavier jacket on the cool, blustery night when I spotted this attractive looking lady standing further down the sidelines from me talking to a girl standing beside her while watching the game. Whenever I would venture a glance her way I could swear that she seemed to be looking right back at me.

Though she was a good distance down the sidelines from me I could see that she had some of the brightest eyes and one of the nicest figures I had ever seen. I had to do my best not to stare, but once when she saw me looking her way she smiled a big, bright, beautiful smile and I felt my pulse quicken a bit. I hadn't been feeling especially well at the time, in fact I was very depressed, so this small bit of interaction with this lovely female was quite exhilarating. As the game progressed, I slowly, unintentionally albeit intentionally, edged my way closer to where she was standing in order to get a better look at her.

When I had first spotted her I had wondered if she might be a mother of one of the boys playing in the game, but as I drew closer I saw that she was probably too young to have a son in this game and I was inwardly pleased because this meant she may still be a single, approachable woman, or fair game as we men like to call it. I spent the rest of the game watching her and the game, positive by this time that she had in fact been watching me before because she had given me a few more big smiles when I had looked her way now that I was closer and there was no doubt in my mind. I smiled back as best I could for a man who hadn't been in the habit of smiling much of late, then went back to watching the game and my son while at the same time wondering who this young lady was as I had never seen her before and this was not a big town at all.

After the game ended and we had all gathered in our young warriors, gallant looking despite mud stained uniforms, we all began walking from the field to the parking lot. My son lagged behind, as he always did, to chatter with his teammates and before I knew it the attractive young lady and I were walking side by side. I said hello to her and asked her if she enjoyed the game. She smiled a big smile and said that she did.

I introduced myself to her and pointed out my son and asked her if she had a son or someone she knew playing on the team. She said her name was April and she was there watching her younger brother play and she pointed out one of the boys walking along with my boy. She said her family had just moved here from New York City and that she was a senior at the high school here. I asked her if she missed NY or if she liked it here better and she said she liked it here because NY was so crazy. Then about that time the boys caught up with us so I told her it was nice to have met her and I wished her good luck in her new surroundings here. I told her I had grown up in this town and it was a nice town.

We didn't really have much of a conversation right there, just a little chitchat as we walked off the field. Though it felt good talking to her there, very good in fact because there seemed to be some chemistry between us, I was disappointed to learn that she was only a senior in high school. I was desperate to meet someone new in my life to wipe away the pain of a failing/failed marriage, but I conceded that this was not going to be the one for me. I was quite an emotional wreck at the time. It was now just a few months past the last, and subsequently final, time my wife had abandoned me. I was a terribly heartbroken man, and the chance meeting of an attractive female paying such attention to me felt nice. Very nice.

And why not, I thought. Why shouldn't I feel nice? I was not a bad guy. I was doing what I felt was the right thing to do at the time. Not just the right thing but the *only* thing to do at the time. I had no choice. I was the one at home with my children taking care of them every day and every night. I was doing what many like me would not. With the term 'dead-beat dad' being tossed about in the news every day, I was one dad who was there for his kids every day -- so why not an angel to answer my prayers?

I was not the one who had broken up my marriage of ten years. I loved my wife dearly and had never wanted to separate or divorce. What can I say? I worshiped my wife. She had been my first, and only, love up to that point. To say she still floated my boat was the understatement of the century. Despite having been a couple for over fifteen years, I still relished every minute I spent with her. She was a superwoman to me, and I considered myself to be the luckiest man on Earth. She was my world and her name was Carolyn...

...CAROLYN

My wife's name was Carolyn. We met in high school, my senior year and her junior. We had been three years in the same school yet I don't believe I had ever noticed her before, but when I saw her one day in study-hall I was blown away. Most people don't believe in love at first sight, but after that day I do. I do because it happened to me. For whatever reason, whatever stars were aligned that day or whatever chemistry was active between us two, when I looked into her eyes that day suddenly the world was a whole different place.

I wasn't exactly in high demand during my high school years. I had a few girls to express interest in me, but I was never interested in them. Seems like I never wanted what I could have and always wanted what I couldn't. For instance, there was one girl in my class who liked me all through high school. She was a popular girl, and attractive and slender and nice, but instead of being attracted to her she just didn't do it for me. I like skinny, mind you, and she was plenty skinny but I just wasn't interested in her in a boyfriend/girlfriend kind of relationship.

But how can one explain what they are attracted to? How can a person who likes red-headed girls explain why it is that the red hair and freckled skin make them more attracted to that person and more interested in being around them? How can a person who likes a girl with thick legs and a hefty backside explain why they feel a stirring within their very soul when such a girl looks at them a certain way? Such things cannot be explained. It is called nature, and I firmly believe that there are some things in nature that science and scientists will never come close to understanding.

So when the sister of a friend of mine came up to me that day in study hall and told me that a girl named Carolyn thought I was cute and wanted to go out with me I said I had no clue who Carolyn was and she told me to turn around because she was seated a few rows behind me and when I did it was all over for me. I saw this girl smiling the most beautiful smile I had ever laid eyes upon, and this beautiful, bright eyed, chocolate skinned girl named Carolyn became a part of my mind, my body, and my soul, and I cannot tell you why but I know I was in love right there at that spot. I must have had a shocked look on my face because Carolyn just kept smiling that beautiful smile at me and I couldn't help but smile back and I must have been a sight to see because I knew I had just died and gone to heaven.

And there she was this beautiful black girl and I as white as snow yet the feelings I felt knew nothing of color nor race nor up or down nor sideways or forwards nor right or wrong, I only knew I felt a fluttering deep inside the pit of my stomach like I had never felt before, and as I walked over to her and we introduced ourselves to each other there in study hall that day I swear my feet never touched the ground once the whole time.

And thus began a whirlwind relationship of sneaking around with each other including many a midnight rendezvous because her father did not approve of her seeing me a white guy and my parents didn't approve of us going out either because it was without the blessing of her parents, and so consequently, Carolyn and I spent the better part of the next two years sneaking around behind their backs seeing each other whenever we could. Many nights I would drive for almost thirty minutes down a curvy country road through valleys and hillsides then turn down a long dead end to meet her. The black community there had sprung up generations ago close to some coal mines located in the mountain and this was where many of the blacks had worked for a living.

Carolyn's parents were hard workers. Her dad was a foreman at the local ammunition plant and her mom cleaned houses in town every day. They always went to bed early and so after they did Carolyn would sneak out of her bedroom window and walk down the dark road to meet me and we would get back on the main road and drive down towards the river to park. There was this special spot where we would pull off the main road, a dirt driveway to an old coal mine long since closed, and we would climb into the back of my mom's station wagon and spend hours back there making out and listening to a radio station out of Chicago, Illinois (WLS I think) that played gospel music late at night. And we would lay there and gaze up at the stars in the sky and listen to the likes of Mahalia Jackson and it would seem as though we were the only people in the world and it was just heaven until we would have to part.

And I would drop her off on her road again and her father would catch her coming in sometimes and punish her severely because he knew she was sneaking around to see me and he wanted it to stop. I absolutely hated causing her father pain and knew I was creating friction between a father and his daughter but I loved his daughter dearly and couldn't understand why he wouldn't just give me a chance. I sometimes wished I could just walk away and make everyone happy, everyone except Carolyn and me. But it was my life, and, fact is, I knew I couldn't stop seeing Carolyn if I wanted to. I absolutely adored her.

So our sneaking around continued. Carolyn's father was a stout man with hard features and a harder attitude. He didn't like me at all despite the honest attempts I had made to show him that I truly cared for his daughter and was not just out to use her as he was sure I was in it for. To him, white men only used black women. He had seen his share of it growing up as he did in the mountains of West Virginia and he did not want his own daughter to be used and then discarded and so he would not give me a chance at all. Although I sympathized with him and understood where he was coming from I did not like the way he generalized about me and white people and so I felt that if sneaking around was the only way I could see his daughter then I was going to do it because I knew my feelings for her were genuine and I knew he would see that one day.

I remember always feeling so bad when I would drop her off on the road after we had been together because I would worry about her making it in without being caught by her dad. He had a heavy hand and he was bound and determined to straighten out his eighteen-year old daughter with brute force alone if that's what it took.

He would be waiting up for her in the dark and when she would come sneaking in through the kitchen door she had left unlocked and he would beat her. She would call me the next day to tell me she had been caught and we would have to wait a few days before we could see each other again. But we would always find a way.

Sometimes she would tell her parents that she was going to ride into town with her cousin or a friend and they would pick her up at her house and always make it a point to say hello to her parents to make it look good. Then I would meet them at some predetermined location and me and Carolyn would go spend a few hours together until I would have to take her back to meet up with her cousin or friend so she could ride home with them. This ruse would last for a while until her father would find out she had been meeting me and he would beat her some more. He was a very hard man. Not a bad man, actually a very good family man was Oscar Sherman, but stern. And he was only trying to protect his daughter because he knew how some white men abused black women in those days.

Sometimes I would take a chance and drive past her house in the dark and meet her at her sister-in-law's house at the very end of the dead-end road. I would park my car up in the woods so it couldn't be easily spotted from the road. Her sister-in-law was very cool about allowing us to meet there. She would go on to bed and leave us alone to do what lovers do. We would spend hours running our fingers over each other's bodies while lying there in the dark. I marveled at how smooth and how warm her skin was, and she always wanted to play with the small tuft of hair that was beginning to grow on my chest.

Sometimes we would hear a car coming up the road and we would hold our breaths as headlights shone through the window and crawled along the wall above us as her father cruised slowly by outside in search of any sign of foul play. As weird as it sounds, it was as exhilarating as it was terrifying to us. I felt so alive being there with her. I was crazy in love and felt I would have to one day stand up to her father if it meant keeping her. And one day I almost did just that.

I was taking her home one summer's night and had just turned onto her dead end road when her father's little VW bug jumped out of the brush and fell in directly behind us headlights on bright. Being a dead end road we were trapped. We both were in a panic as we crawled along not sure what to do, but the only thing we could do was to finally stop the car and face the music. I stopped and her father stopped behind me and got out of his car. Carolyn and me sat there scared to death.

I rolled down my window as her father walked up beside me and calmly placed a pistol to my chest and said if I didn't leave right then he was going to kill me. Furthermore, if he ever caught me with his daughter again he was going to kill me. I looked down at that gun pointing at my chest and I guess I was just drunk from fear and adrenaline flow because it really didn't register with me that I was in any danger. I was in shock.

He told Carolyn to get out and come around the car. He took the pistol away from my chest then dropped her with one punch. I remember sitting there thinking this is not happening it's just a bad dream I'm going to wake right now. This is not happening this is not happening was racing through my mind. I remember half mumbling half babbling something to the effect that I didn't want to leave because he was wrong in thinking that I was only using his daughter and I loved her and I did not like him hitting her that way. He yelled at me to get the hell out of there before he loses his self-control and shoots me, and in my state of shock I told him to shoot me if that is what it would take to prove to him that I loved her.

Everything seemed to be taking place in slow motion, and it was an outer body experience because I was talking and I was hearing myself talk but I didn't feel like it was me talking and I didn't feel like it was me there but rather I felt as if I was just watching the whole episode happen but not to me.

Her father took a step towards me then suddenly the side of my face exploded in pain. Carolyn's older brother Clarence had jumped out of the bushes and punched me square in the jaw. I never saw it coming and never even saw him until after the punch. My face zinged with pain. "*Get out of here white boy, we don't want you down here anymore!*" Clarence screamed at me.

Stunned I slowly focused to see Clarence standing there glaring at me with his fists balled and his father behind him still holding a gun. On the road beside them looking up at me through crying eyes was Carolyn. Dazed, confused, my face throbbing with pain I gently pressed on the accelerator and slowly pulled away. I just slowly, helplessly, shamefully pulled away. I looked in my rear view mirror and I could see Carolyn's father punching her some more when she tried to stand up but I just kept on driving. Tears rolled down my face and their shapes became blurry until they faded into the night but I just kept going. I just kept going.

I was in a daze the whole way home. It felt like my whole world had just come crashing down. I was sick to my stomach thinking about the beating that Carolyn was getting. She was taking all the heat for something we were both responsible for. I felt anger, I felt pain, my heart was still racing from the trauma, but worst of all I felt so damned helpless.

And it didn't help that Carolyn's brother had punched me the way he did. He had always been so nice to me and was always sympathetic towards our predicament, so it hurt me to have him do that and yell at me. But after thinking about it some more I realized that he had undoubtedly saved my life that night. I never for once believed that Carolyn's father would actually shoot me, but perhaps Clarence saw that I was pushing his father over the edge. Months later he apologized to me and confirmed what I thought. Clarence was/is a good guy.

Looking back, a bullet that night would have been merciful compared to the torment Carolyn would later put me through.

I didn't hear from her for a quite some time after that bad scene on the road that night. I later learned from her cousin that Carolyn's parents had been sent away to Baltimore to live with her uncle for a while. It was a long, lonely summer, but when she came back home for the beginning of school again she called me...

...SHE CALLED ME

April called me that weekend after we had first met. I hadn't given her much thought after that first meeting. Actually, that's not true. I did think of her often, but in a wistful sort of way more than anything else. I would think of how she was so bright eyed and attentive when we were talking, and of how beautiful she was. And then I would scold myself for even thinking that this attractive young girl might be the least bit interested in a bore like me.

But then out of the clear blue she called me to talk, and we talked and we laughed and she giggled and I found myself wondering what the hell I was doing talking to this young high school girl like this. But her youthful exuberance reminded me of my wife when I had first met her, and it felt good to talk to her, or at least listen to her talk which is mostly what I did. She would just go on and on about anything. She would be serious one minute and then be silly the next and burst out giggling and I couldn't help but laugh too. I was the captive audience.

Her phone calls became more frequent. She would tell me about school and her friends and how goofy this or that boy is, and who liked her and who didn't. Sometimes she would talk about more serious matters like her home life and her relationship with her mom. She told me that she hated living with her mom and that once she graduated in the spring she was going to move out and get her own place. She said her mom made her do all the housework and that she was too strict on her.

She didn't talk much about life back in New York. I knew she only lived with her mother and not her father. Once, when I asked her about her father she said that he had done some things to her when she was young and that he was in prison for it. I was shocked. I felt sorry for her, and I didn't know what to say so I didn't ask her anymore questions about her father and she never mentioned him again. Her sad story seemed to draw me closer to her. I felt as if she were a young lady who had had a rough go of it and was in need of someone who could rescue her and give her a better life, and I began to feel that perhaps I might be that someone.

And after all, I deserved to have someone didn't I? Didn't I sit at home every night of the week being Mr. Mom *and* Mr. Dad while the rest of the world was out partying and having a good time? Didn't that make me special in a way? The only thing I had to look forward to in life was watching "Twin Peaks" on television once a week. The very essence of my existence at that time was focused on who killed Laura Palmer. Didn't that make me special? If not, what did...?

...WHAT DID

What did make me special, or to rephrase that, what was it that made me think I was special? Stupidity? What was it that ever led me to believe that all my years of underachieving in rural, middle-class America had yielded a diamond in the rough? I knew that I grew up feeling different from many of my classmates. They all seemed to have direction in life, but not me. They all had college plans lain out, but not me. I was not exposed to any of the founding father's philosophies or family traditions growing up. My father was from New Jersey and my mother from New Orleans, so naturally our family settled somewhere between the two in a small southwestern Virginia town. It took two days drive to visit relatives so we did not see our relatives very often.

We lived in a modest neighborhood outside of a college town surrounded on all sides by cow fields. Besides the college, an ammunition plant was the only other big business in the area. The town population was 20,000 people in the summer and twice that during the rest of the year when college was in session.

During my early years, our local college football team was horrible; thus, no one ever heard of the college or knew where it was located. Consequently, the only true claim to fame for the entire area was the fact that the nearby ammunition plant was on Russia's Top Ten Hit List for a nuclear strike in the event of war. It felt good to be from such an important place.

I did not have grandparents around to sit me on their lap and tell me stories about my parents and the stupid things they did when they were my age. Once we stayed with my grandparents in New Jersey for a while because my dad was changing jobs and we were waiting to move into a house or something. I remember my grandparent's apartment was in a high-rise, pane glass covered building. With elevators. The elevators were awesome. We stayed there for about a month I think. I remember climbing all over the couch and watching the neat fish in the giant fish tank and looking out the glass window at the park and getting yelled at by my grandfather a lot. Mostly I remember getting yelled at by my grandfather. And my mother got yelled at a lot by my grandfather too.

I remember my mother crying to my father because we were all cramped up in that apartment and it wasn't us kids' fault that we were breaking all the glass stuff around the place. My grandfather liked to drink and he would get a little tipsy and then terrorize us all at night while we all sat in the living room watching the television. We kids, four of us ages five to newborn, would remain perfectly still until we forgot why we were remaining perfectly still, then we would begin climbing the tables and couches and walls again until my grandfather exploded and we would sit still some more. And on it went day in and day out.

But we made it through that month at my grandparents. I think it was mostly thanks to my grandmother. As rough as my grandfather could be, my grandmother was an angel. She was the exact opposite of what grandpa was. Grandma is soft spoken, kind, and caring. No one could ever understand how she put up with my grandfather. But it was obvious to me that she loved him and needed him; just as my grandfather needed her for someone he could boss around and yell at. But despite his transgressions, I loved him. He was my grandfather. And I bear his name. I am the third, my father the junior. My grandfather wasn't a monster always, and I have found that I inherited many of his distrusts in some of society's institutions such as lawyers, and banks. And in his defense for as long as he was alive he never forgot my children or me on our birthdays. He and my grandmother would always send my kids something on their birthdays. My grandfather could be as soft as he was hard.

Later on in my childhood, when the family took vacations, most of the time we went south to New Orleans to visit my mom's side of the family. I suppose I became closer to my relatives down there, mainly because I did see them every now and then. I loved my Aunt Linda and Uncle Joe, and my three cousins were a good bit younger than me and they absolutely loved to ride on my back, slight of frame as I was. When visiting them, I learned to always keep moving so as to make it difficult for one of them to mount my back. But they still managed to wear me out a time or two.

My cousins would take us around their neighborhood to meet all the kids there. They all seemed to be one big gang, but not like the rough gangs of today's inner cities, no, they were more like a *Little Rascals* type group. I remember one kid was a boxer and he was the most popular kid in the neighborhood. This was like an Irish-Catholic type neighborhood where you might expect to find Mickey Rooney clowning around, or James Cagney picking a fight with someone, except it wasn't in the Bronx of New York but instead in the deep south in a parish of New Orleans Louisiana. It was all so different to me, and exciting, kind of like the exciting feel of a big city with all its neon lights humming and the skyscrapers and the hustle-bustle day and night, but not exactly. This was a different type of excitement, one that enveloped me and held me captive. Or perhaps it was just the heat that swallowed me up.

The heat in New Orleans was like nothing I had ever experienced before -- the heat and the humidity. And we always visited in July and August, the hottest months of the year. I remember sitting outside on the steps of my aunt & uncle's house and feeling like I was suffocating. I would stay outside for brief periods, then rush back inside to the relief of the window air-conditioning unit they had. Boy, did the ice-cold air from that air conditioner feel good. I can't imagine how people ever survived down there without AC. I guess everyone just sat outside on their porches all day and fanned themselves.

After it finally cooled off some outside in the evening, people would venture out of their houses and the local boys would play football in the streets. This was one of the best parts of my vacations there. I loved to play football, so I was a happy camper when I got into the games. I was always fairly thin growing up, so what I lacked in strength I made up for in speed. I wasn't the fastest by any stretch of the imagination, but I wasn't slow either. I could keep up with most, but there was always that occasional one who could blow past me while I was at cornerback. I liked defensive back on defense, and wide out on offense. I loved the game.

And speaking of loving the game, New Orleans is where I learned to play, and love, the card game Hearts. With nothing to do during the hot afternoons but sit around inside my aunt and uncle's house, my aunt taught me hearts. She and my uncle would play regularly with other couples. They played teams, but the game can be played as teams or every man for himself. To this day it is my favorite card game. Hours were spent sitting around their kitchen table playing Hearts.

And to make it even more exciting, we would play a penny a point. This made it a real challenge not to get cleaned out by my uncle who would play with us in the evenings after he got home from working at the bank. He was such a clown, always laughing and joking, especially if he was killing you in hearts. He would laugh and sing and it would just get you so frustrated that you wanted to beat him so bad. He had a big smile and he would just laugh and his eyes would laugh too when he saw you were getting frustrated at losing and he would just keep rubbing it in.

Yes, he was a real clown, except when he was losing at the cards. He took his cards very seriously, and he was very good at them. So, it was a special treat playing against him and trying to beat him. If you did, you really felt as if you did something. It didn't happen often, and for every one game won there were about ten where you would have to endure the laughing and singing and carrying on and you would just want to strangle him strangle him. And all the while my aunt would be there with sympathetic glances and words of encouragement. She was the Ying to his Yang. As angry as my uncle could get me, my aunt could make me feel at ease. They were like a tag team those two, and I loved all those special moments playing Hearts there at my aunt and uncle's. Those are memories I shall cherish for the rest of my life.

And meanwhile back in Blacksburg, the wind moaned softly as it blew over the hills and through the fields of corn and hay, and all the while the yellow birds chirped...

...THE YELLOW BIRDS

He heard chirping sounds coming from somewhere high above his head. Kneeling there on his sidewalk in front of his family's home in the small town neighborhood, the young boy looked up into the clear blue sky, squinting. It was them; the yellow birds. But he already knew that it was. There was no mistaking their chirps because they were always the same. A quick chirp followed by more chirps that started high on the scales then dropped down to fall off the edge. After a second, another quick chirp would be followed by the same chorus. It was like that over and over and over, every time. The young boy could whistle it easily by now.

Nearly blinded by the bright sunlight, he watched as a small flock of six or seven yellow birds crossed the sky high above him. He watched as they each bobbed up and down. What a strange way of flying the young boy always thought. They would flap their tiny black wings and chirp while climbing in altitude, then go silent and stop flapping their wings causing them to drop. The suddenly, they would vigorously flap their tiny wings again and chirp and climb. This strange, dyslexic pattern always mesmerized the young boy. It seemed spastic, yet at the same time it was fluid and harmonic all at the same time. He continued to watch as the birds flew high above and disappeared over the fields behind his house.

The young boy stood there for a moment staring off into the distant sky as if in a trance. Slowly, he looked down to turn his attention back to the grasshopper he had pinned to the sidewalk between his index finger and thumb. The grasshopper was trying to turn his head as if to bite the fingers that held him down, and its legs squirmed frantically.

In the other hand the young boy held a magnifying glass which he meticulously raised and lowered in order to focus an intensified beam of sunlight shining through into a tiny dot of concentrated energy. This blinding dot of sparkling, white heat was focused squarely atop the grasshopper's twisting head. The young boy's face was a picture of concentration as he held the magnifying glass perfectly still until the white dot began to crackle and pop, and then smoke. The grasshopper kicked its legs frantically, but to no avail- the young boy's grip was too firm. The grasshopper's tiny head jerked about while it crackled and smoked, and a black goo began to ooze from its mouth. After a moment the grasshopper stopped moving, its head a smoking black nub.

The young boy could never stand the repugnant smell of the burning grasshoppers. The stench was always the same. Yucky, he thought! He stood up and carelessly tossed the dead grasshopper out into the street in front of his house, then dashed inside. A few moments later he emerged with his BB rifle and headed for the fields in search of the yellow birds.

The young boy crossed through a vacant lot and came to a dirt road that cut through the fields and off into the distance for as far as the eye could see. He set out down the dirt road. It was a hot summers day and the young boy was spending it much like he had spent most other days of this summer. If he wasn't burning up things with his magnifying glass, he was hunting the yellow birds in the fields behind his house. Walking down the dirt road, the young boy looked all around. New homes were going up everywhere. There were vacant lots on either side of the dirt road that were in one phase or another of construction. During the week, crews of carpenters and laborers worked on the new homes. Hammers pounded and bulldozers growled. Some of the lots were only concrete slabs, and some were framed houses under roof. Today was a Sunday and all was quiet. The young boy passed the construction site by and walked further down the road where there was only tall grass and weeds on either side of the road. He walked on with BB gun in hand and nary a care in the world.

****

"Go, go, go, go," yelled the young man above the loud whine of the whirling helicopter blades. His men crouched down under the spinning blades as they waited in line to board the chopper. The young man stood by the open side of the helicopter and helped each of his men clamber up into its belly. As leader of Charlie Company, it was his responsibility to keep things moving at a steady clip. They had just received orders to join the front lines, and they were on their way. It could be the first taste of combat for all the men of Charlie Company, including their leader. The young man shouted "Move it, move it!" above the loud whine of the helicopter blades. When the last of his men were aboard, the young man hopped in and the helicopter slowly lifted off of the runway, hovered momentarily, banked slightly, and then moved off towards the horizon.

The men removed their helmets and sat down on them. The young man looked around at all of his men. All were young men just like him. All were good men too. And all were scared, just like him. He could tell they were scared because their eyes were wide as saucers and they didn't even realize it, a result of intense fear mixed with heightened nerves. The young man was doing all he could to fight back his own crippling fears. He refused to let it wear him down and paralyze him. His men depended on him to lead, and he would be damned if he was going to let them down.

As the helicopter flew on towards the front lines, the men of Charlie Company sat on their helmets and stared off into space. It's hard to say what goes through a young man's mind right before he goes off into battle. Some think about their wives or girlfriends back home; some think of their childhood; some think of their mom and dad, sisters and brothers, lovers and friends; and some think of killing while some think of dying. The young man thought of the target village and of the reconnaissance photos he had studied.

****

The young boy came to a tall mound of dirt that a bulldozer had made while leveling out the road. Around the base of the mound were scattered plastic and glass pieces everywhere. This mound of dirt was the young boy's practice range. He used it to shoot anything and everything from empty tin cans and bottles to his plastic models that he had painstakingly assembled just the year before. *Frankenstein, The Mummy, Wolfman* and *The Thing* had all fallen victims to the young boy's deadly aim. The young boy rummaged through a carnage of plastic body parts strewn about and picked up a piece of what appeared to have once been someone's leg, probably *Frankenstein's*. He placed the plastic piece a little ways up on the earthen mound, then backed away and paced off ten giant steps from the mound. He turned, slowly raised the BB gun to level to his eye, took aim, and fired. The dirt just beside the plastic leg jumped. The young boy adjusted his aim ever so slightly and fired again. This time he was just a little high.

Steady. Adjust. His third shot hit home. The young boy spent the next half an hour shooting at various pieces he could find large enough to shoot at. Then he became bored and set off back down the road in search of the yellow birds.

As he walked his footsteps kicked dust up from the road. It was a hot day, and the weeds in the field were so high that they blocked off any breeze that may have blown across the road. The young boy could hear crickets chirping in the fields and he saw butterflies and bees flying everywhere. A rabbit jumped from the weeds and darted across the road in front of the young boy, startling him. The young boy quickly regained his composure and was able to pop off a quick shot at the fleeing rabbit. He missed. The rabbit was much too fast and quickly disappeared in the tall weeds. It was gone before the young boy could pop off another shot at it. The young boy wondered if he could actually kill a rabbit with his BB gun. He figured he would have to shoot it in the eye or through the ear to kill it His friend had a CO2 pellet rifle. It was a real beauty. It could kill a rabbit for sure the young boy thought. But not this BB gun. The young boy was going to ask Santa Claus for a CO2 gun just like his friends this Christmas.

****

Charlie Company's mission was to "secure" a small village in the Delta Quadrant where there were reports of guerilla activity. Reconnaissance photos barely showed the enemy village nestled in dense jungle. Charlie Company was being airlifted to a safe landing zone from where they would hike a couple of hours through the jungle to the enemy village and secure it. "Expect heavy resistance," headquarters had warned. This was a real humdinger for a first mission thought the young man. Some may not make it out. Perhaps him.

"Check your weapons!" barked the young man. His men each propped their rifles upright in front of where they sat and they examined their weapons from top to bottom. The young man pulled the ammunition clip from his rifle, looked it over then re-inserted it with an audible 'click.' Then, in a few seconds time he re-calibrated his scope. The young man was good with his weapon. He was, by far, the best marksman of Charlie Company.

He looked at his men to make sure they were going over their weapons. They were all doing as they had been instructed. These really are good men thought the young man. They listen well and do as I tell them. And this was because the men respected the young man and they looked up to him. The young man was a crack shot and his men admired this. They put their faith in the young man, despite the fact that he had never seen live combat either. The war was not going well for their side and there were not enough experienced veterans to lead the inexperienced troops. The young man was the best choice for Charlie Company, no question.

****

The young boy walked down the road popping off quick shots at anything that moved. Mostly bees. He especially loved to shoot the fat, slow moving bumblebees. He could just see their round black & yellow bodies exploding in a green *splat* in midair, but it never happened that way. The bumblebees would always dart to one side or the other and dodge the incoming BB. They seemed to have some sort of invisible force field around them. The young boy figured that they must have very keen senses and that a BB must look like a large bowling ball to them. But this did not stop the young boy from trying anyway.

The young boy walked on. He stopped walking for a moment to listen for the yellow birds. The birds only chirped when they flew, so they were very hard to find unless they were in flight. Sometimes they would be perched on the tops of bushes in the field and the young boy would be walking along and still not see them until he was nearly on top of them and then they would quickly fly away.

It was impossible for him to shoot them out of the air while they flew. The yellow birds were only a little larger than a hummingbird, and nearly as quick it seemed. They were beautiful birds with bright yellow bodies, black wings, and a small black plume atop their head that looked like a hat. The young boy had only gotten a good look at them close up a few times. They were very fidgety birds by nature and did not like to sit still for very long at all. Whenever he had been close enough for a possible shot, the barely perceptible sound of the BB's rolling around inside of his rifle would be enough to send the birds scattering. To get a really good look at the birds the young boy had to sit motionless and watch. They were magnificent birds thought the young boy. So quick. So agile. So beautiful. So challenging. The young boy wanted so badly to shoot one, to conquer it as one might a rival. The young boy kicked up some dust with a grungy looking sneaker and then continued on down the road.

****

The young man felt the helicopter begin its decent. He looked down to see a field below surrounded by forest. He shouted to his men to put their helmets on and get ready to move. "This is it," he went on, "stay low and stay alert!" The helicopter hovered momentarily above the ground, then set down abruptly. The young man was the first out, followed quickly by his men. The grass leaned over and rippled from the force of the helicopter's spinning blades and the men ran over it and into the cover of taller weeds. Once the men were all out, the helicopter rose quickly into the afternoon sky, banked, and disappeared over the treetops. The thumping noise of its blades reverberated loudly, then grew more distant until all was dead silent for the men crouching there in the field.

The young man studied the forest line for any sign of the trouble. Seeing nothing, he motioned for his men to follow. They all dashed swiftly through the tall grass and into the forest. Once inside and under the cover of the trees, the young man got his bearings using his compass and map. Using hand signals, the young man instructed his men to follow behind him single file and Charlie Company set out for the enemy village.

The young man picked his way through the dense foliage with his men in tow. He signaled for his men to halt. Progress was slow and arduous. The young man would constantly signal an abrupt halt to listen and scan for any sign of trouble. The men not only had to keep a look out for the enemy on the ground, they had to look out for snipers hiding up in the trees as well. Snipers were Charlie Company's biggest fear. Rays of sunshine breaking through billowy clouds in the sky and cascading down through gaps in the canopy above gave the forest a surreal, enchanting glow and also made it difficult to see. Lines and angles became distorted by the ever changing light and shadows. So beautiful, so magical, yet so deadly thought the young man.

They were falling behind schedule, but the young man did not want to get in a hurry and make a mistake. And a mistake out here meant death. The young man was being overcautious, yet he could not help but feel uneasy. He wanted to think it was a case of nerves, but something else was bothering him and he could not put his finger on it. Every now and then he would think he could hear a sound, like a tinkling or whistling sound, and it would send a chill up his spine. But when he stopped to listen, he could hear nothing. Just silence.

The young man stood surveyed their surroundings one last time, then, detecting no danger, signaled for Charlie Company to resume its trek towards the village.

****

Off in the distance the young boy spotted a large bird sitting on a power line that stretched across the field. It looked to be a white-tailed dove from its size. The young boy took aim at the bird and fired. The bird didn't flinch, well out range of the BB gun. The young boy crouched low and entered the tall weeds in an attempt to sneak up on the bird. He had only gone a few steps when the bird leapt from the wire and flew away. The young boy shot at it, but it was no chance. The young boy did not care. He was not after that big bird. It was slow and lazy and would be easy to kill. He wanted one of the little yellow birds with the black wings and the magical way of flying. They were the real prizes. They were his quest.

The young boy came to a fork in the dirt road and he followed the road that lead down a hill and looped around until it ended beside a large, old tree. Sometimes the yellow birds would rest on the branches of the old tree or on the bushes around it. He walked down the hill and approached the tree slowly, surveying all around to see if he could spot a yellow bird. There were no birds. The young boy raised his gun and aimed at a large monarch butterfly that was fluttering above a sunflower. He fired. The butterfly jerked upward, then swiftly fluttered away.

The young boy decided to wait a while in the shade of the tree to see if any of the yellow birds would come by. It was a hot day and the shade felt good. He sat by the side of the road. With a stick he traced pictures of army tanks and jets in the dirt. After a while he skipped stones down the road, or bounced them off the trunk of the old tree. All the while he kept a sharp lookout for the birds, but they never showed. The young boy grew tired of waiting. He was getting hungry now so he decided to head back home.

Just as he started back up the hill he heard them approaching. He crouched low as four of the yellow birds flew overhead and landed on bushes not far from where he stood. The young boy didn't move a muscle as he watched the four birds play. Though he was very close to them, the birds did not seem to notice the young boy at all. Or if they did, they sensed no danger. As the young boy stood there preparing to act, one of the little yellow birds flew off and was followed quickly by another. Now only two birds leapt from bush to bush.

****

After having walked for close to two hours now, the young man now had the uneasy sensation that they were being watched. Nerves young man nerves he thought, because they were getting nearer to the village. Yet, he just could not shake the disconcerting feeling that easily. He raised his hand and made a tight fist, the signal for his men to freeze. The young man crouched down slowly and his men did the same behind him. They all scanned the jungle up and down with darting eyes. The young man used his keen vision to peer into and through the dense foliage. He saw nothing.

Convinced that it was only a case of nerves, the young man had just raised up and signaled to proceed when his eye caught movement in the trees up ahead and he dropped quickly and silently to the ground and his men did the same behind him.

In the trees dead ahead about fifty yards sat a sniper. The young man watched from behind a bush as the sniper turned his head in all directions, as if he had heard something and was searching for its source. Good thought the young man, the sniper had not spotted them yet.

The young man pointed out the sniper for his men, then motioned for them to stay down and out of sight. Using hand signals he informed his men that he was going to take the sniper out with one shot.

The young man sat still for some time, all the while scanning the dense forest for other snipers that might be in waiting. He spotted none. The young man figured the sniper was a lookout for the village and had most probably been asleep when Charlie Company happened upon him. Their movement or a stray sound may have awoken the sniper. Whichever, the sniper was still looking all around. Sometimes it seemed as if he were looking right at Charlie Company, but he did not see them. The young man was thankful their green camouflage uniforms blended well with the jungle.

He studied the sniper. The sleeveless brown shirt he work and his dark skin blended him in well with the tree. The young man was not sure how he had spotted the sniper before the sniper had spotted him, but he knew he had been very lucky in having done so. One in a million chance. And from here the sniper was an easy target for the young man, a deadly marks man. Million to one chance he couldn't miss.

The young man's heart pounded inside his chest as he ever so quietly removed his rifle silencer from his ammunition belt. He slowly and methodically screwed it onto the end of his rifle. The men of Charlie Company all watched in admiration as their leader meticulously prepared for the kill. They had seen the young man pick fruit off of trees from twice this distance before, so they knew this would be an easy target for him. The only thing in doubt was whether the young man would shoot the sniper through the heart, or through the eye. The young man smiled at his men and winked. He gave the silencer one last firm twist.

****

The two remaining birds continued to play with each other, leaping from bush to bush. The young boy's heartbeat pounded as he slowly brought the rifle up to his shoulder, careful as to not allow the BB's inside to roll around and alert the birds. He aimed at his target. One yellow bird sat atop a bush and twitched its head back and forth nervously causing the branch it sway. The young boy's hands trembled as he lined up his shot. He had been in this position before, but had always missed. He watched as the bird flicked its head and fluttered its wings as if to take off, but it didn't. The bush swayed even more. The young boy held his breath to steady his aim and ever so gently squeezed the trigger. Just at the very moment, the yellow bird turned its head to look directly at the young boy. The BB gun fired.

Instantly the bush seemed to jump and a small bird darted out and flew away. It quickly disappeared into the field. The young boy watched it fly away and his heart sank a bit. But there had been two birds and he was almost positive that only one bird had gotten away. It all happened so fast that he could not be sure.

His heart pounded as he raced the short distance to the bush. His eyes quickly scanned the bush and the ground under it but he did not see anything and his entire body sagged as he thought he had missed again.

And then he saw it.

A tiny little ball of fir lay nestled in between some blades of grass. The young boy's heart skipped a beat as he thought it might be the yellow bird. He kneeled down and gently parted the grass with his fingers and there it was- the yellow bird.

The young boy gently scooped the yellow bird up into his palm. Its body was limp and its head flopped to the side in the young boy's hand. The young boy studied his conquest.

The yellow coat that once seemed so bright was now dull, as if a light had been turned off from within. Three tiny droplets of red blood were spattered on the bird's neck. What had once been pure, dazzling energy was now lifeless and still. The young boy stood there holding the bird and he began to wonder what he had just done.

After weeks upon weeks of hunting the yellow bird, this was not how the young boy thought it would be. What he held in his hand was no majestic prize, no monumental achievement. The elusive yellow bird that he thought would be such a beautiful prize was nothing more than a lifeless ball of fir. The young boy did not feel a great relief or satisfaction as he thought he would. He had finally won, finally conquered that yellow bird, but the cost of his victory was this tiny life he had taken away.

The young boy held the bird to his chest and sobbed uncontrollably. After a short time the young boy buried the yellow bird there under the big tree and then he walked home slowly with his shoulders sagging and his strong little heart broken in two.

****

Tiny beads of perspiration covered the young man's forehead as he brought his rifle up to take aim. He watched the sniper squatting on the tree branch through his rifle scope. He lowered the scope's crosshairs onto the sniper's chest, then directly over his heart. Just as he did, the young man heard that faint whistling sound again, and just then the young man recognized it. It was not a whistle but a chirp. It sounded like the chirps of the yellow birds that he used to hunt years ago when he was a young boy.

And as the young man was momentarily distracted by the sound of his yellow birds, a ray of sunlight cascaded down from an opening in the clouds and the forest's canopy to shine directly on the sniper, bathing him in a brilliant yellow glow. And at that very same moment the sniper turned his head and looked directly at the young man and suddenly the young man flashed back to a little yellow bird he had killed one day in a field when he was a young boy, and he froze. He just froze.

And in the mere millisecond it took for the sniper to bring his weapon up and pop off a quick burst at the young man, the young man remained suspended in time, oblivious to all else except a precious little yellow bird staring directly into his eyes. And as he kneeled there a silent, solitary bullet, headed straight towards the young man traveling in slow motion as if it were floating through the vacuum of a fluctuation in time and space continuum and disappeared into the young man's forehead directly between his eyes forming a small, nearly imperceptible hole then after only a few seconds, yet what seemed to be a lifetime, it suddenly exploded out of the back of his skull sending flecks of brain and tissue matter flying everywhere as it violently exited.

The force of the shot sent the young man sprawling backwards. He lay on the ground and stared straight upwards with wide, blank eyes, and in the precious few seconds it took for him to die, a young boy walked through a field for eternity with BB gun in hand and nary a care...

...CARE

but who really cares,
who is willing to try,
to save a world
that is destined to die

...lyrics from a song off of the late Marvin Gaye's album *What's Going On*. A fantastic album, my favorite of all time I think. It came out in the late sixties or early seventies during the Vietnam War and it has a nice theme of peace and harmony with the Earth. I remember listening to that album over and over while playing cards in the downstairs recreation room of our home during one summer when I was in my early teens. There were about five or six of us guys from the neighborhood that loved to play cards, or gamble rather, and sometimes we would have even more than that playing and we would have to have two separate games going at different tables. We played poker and five-card knock rummy while listening to stuff like Motown's 64 Greatest Hits, The Grass Roots, and The Four Seasons and others that don't come quickly to mind, but my favorite album had to have been Marvin Gaye's with its driving melodies and powerful lyrics about troubled times and the ecology. The Vietnam War was in its full fury, the violent Civil Rights confrontations were winding down, nuclear fallout was a hot topic, and us guys played cards and whooped it up planets away from the suffering and despair. But to me there was something about that album that sunk into my bones, and I began to wonder why things were the way they were and why they didn't seem to ever get better.

And I must have been at a stage in my life where I was very impressionable, and I saw the killing and death from Vietnam on our big color console television and in the pages or our *Life* magazine and I couldn't help by be moved by what I saw. And while all that was going on in the other side of the globe, all these helpless black people were being beaten by police clubs and sprayed with fire hoses in cities here at home, and somewhere along the way I developed a deep empathy for the oppressed and powerless, and I grew to dislike the way things were in society because I saw then that, basically, people are fucked up, and I could not understand what it was that would possess one person to take the life of another simply because of a difference of opinion. I could not fathom this.

And as I grew older I learned that people most often kill people because someone has something that they want, so they kill to get it, and I learned that the bigger a power was the more gluttonous it became until it had to squash anything that got in the way of its quest for food and survival. And I wondered why it was that America was so high and mighty and yet some of its people were starving to death in its cities, and then beaten down by the law if they protested or complained.

I guess it was during those formative years that I developed an affinity towards black people and an aversion towards bigotry and elitism. And to this day I still dislike elitism.

It seems that everyday more people in America are finding it tougher to survive. Unemployment is on the rise while the spending power of the dollar bill decreases. Yet, the elitists still get theirs. In fact, they take more and more every day because they have the power.

But who really cares, who is willing to try...

And then I watch the six o'clock news and I see that the wind is blowing in the Atlantic Ocean and the weatherman is all over it with the latest in wind speed and direction and minute to minute details.

And all along the eastern seaboard a storm warning has been issued because there is a breeze blowing in the tropics. And then it hits me why I am such a negative person: it is because to be positive is to feel that everything is ok, I'm ok you're ok, and to go with the flow would mean to rush out and purchase plywood to shore up all my windows because the most accurate sensors in the world detected a slight increase in wind velocity while Pamela Sue Anderson was blowing in Tommy Lee's ear.

Storm warning! Batten down the hatches mates.

And it pisses me off that this country is so capable and able yet so ignorant and elitist.

So again I ask myself, why can't I just go with the flow? What is it that makes me think I am so special and must act differently from the rest? Is it just to get attention? No, I tell you the reason I felt different from every one else growing up is that I cared about the world when it seemed that no one else around me did. It seemed to me that the entire world was a bunch of fucked up, greedy, lazy pigs, and I was the only one who gave a damn about my brother and my neighbor. I always wanted to swim upstream because by swimming downstream I was falling in with everyone else and saying that everything was just peachy-keen when it wasn't. I followed the beat of a different drummer because following the beat everyone else did meant being in the wrong army fighting for the wrong cause.

Everywhere I looked the country had problems, but did anyone seem to give a damn? I remember where I was the day that President JFK was assassinated. I remember being quickly herded out of the living room, by my mother, and into the back bedroom away from the television that was showing blurry replays of President Kennedy's car driving in a parade and the President is waving and suddenly he slumps to the side. And then a guy in the front seat is trying to climb into the back to shield the President with his body.

Dallas TX is where that occurred. The President was shot in the head by a man who was a paid assassin of some powerful people in

Washington D.C. The President was shot and killed *not* because he had fucked up in the Bay of Pigs and had almost brought about atomic world war, *not* because he was sleeping with Marilyn Monroe on the side, *not* because he was Catholic, but rather *because* he was sympathetic to the Civil Rights Movement of the time. The President of these United States was assassinated because he was working to help the poor and oppressed, namely the black man. Same for his brother Bobby Kennedy – killed because he was sympathetic to the civil rights movements at the time.

And this, if nothing else, is what set me apart from the maddening crowds, it was because I saw how fucked up people everywhere were in their treatment of people with darker skin, and it made me almost feel like an alien...

...ALIEN

I must be an alien, from another planet like David Bowie was. I felt different in high school, what with everyone oohing and aahhing over the blonde haired Marilyn Monroe and red headed Ann Margaret lookalikes, I always felt myself more attracted to the dark haired Diana Rosses and Diane Carols of the world.

I don't know if it was the images on our black-and-white television of the civil rights marches during the late 60's and the police beatings and dog attacks on the crowd of black people, or the soulful sounds of the Supremes or the Jackson Five or Marvin Gaye coming out of Motown, or maybe just hearing that horrible word 'nigger' once too many times, whatever it was I felt differently and thought differently than the guy next to me and I became an alien.

I was an alien when I was working for the bank service company in the nearby city of Roanoke, VA shortly after graduating from high school. I had a job working in the mail room on the evening shift. I remember working with a lot of good people who were very nice to me, including my boss. Carolyn stopped by one evening and everyone met her and was very nice to her. But the following month when time came for the company Christmas Party my boss pulled me aside and said that his bosses at the main office in Richmond wouldn't want me to bring my black girlfriend to the Christmas Party. He said he could not tell me what to do it was my decision but he said it would not look good on me if I was to bring her. I was shocked, but then not really. I asked myself who are these people and where do they come from? The looked like me with their blonde hair and blue eyes, they talked like me with their monotone voices, but they didn't think like me. Not at all.

I took her to the Christmas Party. She was to only black person there. She looked stunning in her red dress and was the prettiest girl there. All the chubby wives of the bank executives were cordial to her but I was afraid they were going to swallow her up as they surrounded her at the salad bar. They smiled and spoke but you could tell people weren't happy she was there. I could see the Richmond execs glaring from their tables. Needless to say I didn't stay at that job long after that.

And I was an alien when I had gotten an apartment near my job there in Roanoke in a town called Vinton, and Carolyn came to visit for a few days. After she had left I was called by the apartment complex's main office and asked to come in because the apartment complex manager wanted to talk to me. I went to the main office and the manager, a lady, told me that some of my neighbors had complained about the company that I kept. Evidently my girlfriend had sat outside on the front steps of the apartment building one evening when I was at work and she had a cigarette and some people saw her and were scared that she was there. *"Oh my God, there's a nigger in our complex!"*

I couldn't believe what crap was coming out of this lady's mouth, but it was. She told me they kept a nice family-oriented apartment complex there and they did not want it to become a hangout for thugs or criminals, or any other undesirables who may threaten the safety of the community and its children.

I kept my cool despite the disdain all over the lady's face when I told her that this girl was my girlfriend and I could vouch for her. I calmly told the lady she had no right to tell me who I can and can't bring into my apartment. She told me yes she could and asked that I not bring my friend around anymore unless I wanted to be evicted. I could see that this lady was not worth wasting another breath on, so I simply got up and walked out of the office. The nerve of her. She looked like a bleach-blonde slob from a trailer park and my girlfriend was trim and healthy and beautiful and here was this red-necked bitch believing she was better than my girlfriend whom she had never even met simply because she was white. Who was this lady? What planet was she from? No, what planet am I from?

Looking back I suppose I could have sued the heck out of the apartment complex, but lawsuits weren't the rave at that time so I loaded up my car and moved my stuff and myself back home to my mom's. The apartment complex tried to try to get me to honor the lease agreement I had signed. They called and threatened *me* with court action a few times, but I merely laughed at them and told them to take me to court and we'll talk about it there. After a few months they finally gave up trying to take my money -- and rightfully so. Who were these people? What planet were they from?

And I was an alien when my wife and I were on vacation at the beach. My mother would babysit our boys every summer thus allowing us to vacation alone. We usually went to the beach for a long weekend, either Nags Head where it was very laid back and relaxing, or Myrtle Beach for the clubs and nightlife. One time at Nags Head we were coming out of a shop when a car full of buttermilk rednecks (a nicer way of saying big, fat ugly rednecks) passed by and one of the fellows stuck his head out the window and shouted "*nigger lover*!" at me. It really pissed me off and I wanted to pick up a rock and hurl it at them but they were long gone before I could blink. Hit and run racists. Typical.

Who were these guys? What planet were they from? Or rather, what planet am I from?

And I was an alien after my marriage had fallen apart I was lonely and so I placed a classified ad in the 'Possibilities' section of the local newspaper, the section where all the lonely hearts look for love, and I called up the newspaper classified ads department on the phone and placed an order for an ad to run in their 'Possibilities' section that says SWM (Single White Male) ISO (In Search Of) SBF (Single Black Female). SWM ISO SBF. This is what I requested for the ad to read along with my preferences to be dark hair, dark eyes.

When the ad ran it ran like this: SWM ISO SF with dark hair and dark eyes. Nothing about SBF. I called the newspaper to inform them that they misprinted the ad but they told me they would not run the ad as I had requested due to their policies. I thought this very strange considering my ad was right above another ad that read SWM ISO Same (Same means Same). I asked the lady you mean to tell me that your paper will run an ad for gays seeking gays but won't run a personal's ad for interracial dating? She replied yes that is their policy.

After a few more phone calls to the paper and its management I finally got them to concede and run my ad as I wished. It was a bit frustrating to have to explain to them that I wanted an interracial ad run, as if there was something not right about it. After threatening to go to the ACLU they said they would run the ad like I wanted. When the next 'Possibilities' ran in the paper my ad read SWM ISO SBF, prefer long blonde hair.

I know they placed the long blonde hair in the ad to humiliate me. I called them and cursed them out and told them to drop the ad I wasn't going to pay for it. They insisted I pay but I told them to shove it and I never heard back from them.

Who were they? What planet were they from?

And alas, going way back, I guess I was even an alien among my family too because my uncle from New Orleans would casually refer to the blacks living in the city's projects as niggers. It was simply the way people talked there. But my mother who was raised in New Orleans did not allow that word in our home and I guess she must have said something to her sister one time when we were visiting them because I never heard my uncle use the word again. Years later when I showed my aunt and uncle a picture of my black girlfriend they said she was a very beautiful girl and asked that I please bring her by so they could meet her. And even later in life they came by to visit me and Carolyn when they were traveling through Virginia on a family vacation. It meant a lot to me.

So just where am I from?

When I was married I felt it was us against them, me and Carolyn and our boys against the rest of the world. I moved about freely amongst people, worked with them, played with them, laughed and cried with them, but through it all I always felt that deep down inside I was different. I can't say why, it's not like I wanted to be, I just was. It was just me.

Perhaps I always wanted to be different so that I could leave an impression...

...IMPRESSION

And God always knew
how badly I had wanted
to make an impression in life
and how I strove for perfection--
but was never even close.

So he followed me up to the cliff that day
and I stood on the edge
where I could see far across the ocean
and it was such a beautiful sight to see.

And then I looked down
at the beach far, far below me
and I stood there
frozen
for what seemed
an eternity.

And then God spoke
and he said to me
"Jump
and you will leave
an impression -
in the sand."

And I walked back home and
ever since that day
I have not thought much
of making
an impression
in life
anymore
...

…ANYMORE

I don't want to play this game anymore. I was rummaging through my closet today and ran across a *capias* and my shoulders slumped. A capias is a legal document that summons a person to appear before a judge right away. Essentially, it is a summons and arrest warrant all in one. How nice.

When I was originally arrested the charge against me was Aggravated Sexual Battery. This was an especially serious charge, perhaps a Class II felony that would mean I had used brute force to sexually molest an underage girl against her wishes.

This capias that I found in my closet had been issued six months after my original arrest and original charge. On this particular capias the prosecutor, or Commonwealth's Attorney as they are known in the Commonwealth of Virginia, was adding on a charge of Indecent Liberties against me. Nothing more had taken place between me and the young girl, no contact whatsoever, I was working every day and going about my business as best I could trying to raise two children on my own yet here I was being charged with more.

I did not understand how the Commonwealth's Attorney could add another charge against me so I swallowed my pride and called an attorney. I asked him why the prosecutor added another charge against me out of the blue and he said that the prosecutor was perfectly within his legal rights to add more charges against me as he sees fit at any time before my trial. He said that it was a legal strategy known as *'piling on.'* He explained that *'piling on'* was used by prosecutors when the case was shaky and the prosecutor needs more ammunition for his side to work with. He said that when there is only one charge against a defendant and the evidence is sketchy, a jury will be reluctant to convict a person of that charge, especially a serious charge when there is a hint of doubt in their mind. And if you cannot find a person guilty beyond a reasonable doubt, then you must find them innocent.

However, by piling up a long list of charges of varying degree against a person, a prosecutor knows that a jury that is reluctant to convict a person of a severe crime will oft times find a defendant guilty of a lesser charge because they feel there is some punishment required. Hence, *'piling on'*. So now I was charged with a severe degree of felony and a lesser charge as well, albeit still a felony.

I can't actually remember being brought before the judge for this *capias*. I think it was all just a formality to them. So not only was I charged with brutally assaulting a young girl but I was also charged with taking indecent liberties with her as well. The state's prosecutor was out to get me and this was another way for him to do it. I wondered was it just me or did he do this frequently...

...FREQUENTLY

After I had first met April, she began calling me quite frequently. I guess she got my last name from her brother and found my number in the phone book. The first call was on the weekend after we had met, and I must admit it was nice to hear from her. I was feeling very down at the moment because my ex-wife had walked out on me and the boys again, so talking to this young attractive lady was very much a boost for me. We chatted for about an hour I believe, and most of the conversation was about her and her friends and what boys like her and a little about New York where she was from. It grew late and she said she had to go so we hung up.

I remember feeling mixed emotions after the call. I didn't go out much and sat at home brooding a lot, so it sure felt good to converse with someone. And the fact that she was a beautiful young lady didn't hurt either. But I had to remind myself that she as a high school student and I was in my early thirties and I was crazy to think that we could be something, so I relished the friendly conversation for just that: a friendly conversation.

She called again the next weekend and we talked some more. I hadn't seen her at all since the first meeting, but here she was calling me again and once again it felt good. Like before, our conversation didn't consist of much substance, and it was very one-sided with her doing most of the talking, but I was content to just sit there on the kitchen floor and listen to this girl go on about her life.

Her calls became more frequent.

Sometimes we would talk about my estranged wife. She had left me to move in again with her eighteen year-old crack cocaine dealing boyfriend, and April could not believe that my wife would leave me and the boys the way she did. She said my wife must be crazy.

She would tell me how she liked my hair and my eyes, and that she felt more attracted to a white man than she did to a black. She told me that she had had a white boyfriend before but he and his family had moved away and it hurt her. She said there was this black boy at school who liked her a lot and they would go out together and do things, but she liked him just as a friend and not a boyfriend and he could not understand this. I was beginning to really like talking with this girl.

She would talk about her best friend sometimes. Her best friend was pregnant at the time, and April would say she wanted to get pregnant and have a baby just like her best friend. She told me that she had had an abortion once and that she regretted it and would never have another. I found myself growing closer and closer to her every time we talked. I began waiting for her call at night after I had put the boys to bed. It became something I would look forward to. I began to believe that perhaps I would have a new love in my life, a new girl who was pretty, and young, and who cared about me. I knew I was much older, but I also knew that it happens.

One time she told me how much she hated school and that she couldn't wait to graduate. She said that she was going to move out of her mothers place after graduation and get an apartment with some other girlfriends. She talked like the plans were already in the works. I thought about how nice it would be for her to move in with me and the boys, but I didn't say this to her. It was still too early in our relationship to be jumping to conclusions like that, and there were lots of issues to consider like our age difference, and like the boys. I wasn't going to just push someone on them without talking to them about it first and getting some feedback.

Then one weekend afternoon April and a girlfriend of hers appeared at my door. In all our conversations on the phone I never once asked her over or had even in any way come on to her. All our dialogue to this point had been on a just-friends level, and I did not feel that it was my place to try to encourage her to have an interest in me considering our ages.

I recall that there were times when I wondered what I was doing talking to her because she was so much younger, but then again she was of legal age and she was soon to be eighteen and out of school and to me she a young woman. I knew she wasn't quite eighteen yet, but she had a birthday coming up and would be very shortly. And I knew that in years past girls were considered to be women and married frequently at age sixteen, so the fact that April was only seventeen soon to be eighteen didn't really bother me too much because she seemed mature to me.

But the fact was that it did bother me some. And not trying to win this young girl over probably did me in because if there is one thing that I have learned in the world of romance and love it is that people are always more attracted to someone who ignores them then they are someone with someone who chases them. So by being indifferent in my conversations with this girl, I probably only made her want me more unfortunately.

So here was April and her friend standing there at my door and it was a quiet Sunday afternoon and I was home watching football or something on TV so I invited them in. We spent the next hour talking in my living room. I studied April, as this was the first time I had seen her since the first time at the ballgame, but I now felt I knew her because of our conversations on the phone. She still looked damn good, even better than I had remembered. If fact, she looked like a goddess, and I found I liked being next to her.

And while I was checking her out I was aware of her doing the same to me. She watched me with clear, bright eyes that seemed to like me watching her. The conversation varied between football and school and boys and I don't remember what else, but it was just small talk while she and I just looked at each other while her friend watched us.

Their visit was over before it began, and when they left I hated to see her go. I checked out her figure as she walked away (as men are prone to do) and she really looked good. She really looked good and I thought that perhaps my luck was going to change thanks to this beautiful young princess with lovely brown eyes...

...LOVELY BROWN EYES

My ex-wife had lovely brown eyes. Beautiful, big brown eyes the color of dark mahogany. So dark that looking into them was like looking into a pair of bottomless pits, and when I looked into them I would simply fall in. I would melt with her eyes and melt with her smile, and then she would have her way with me and I was helpless to resist.

We would spend hours lying next to each other gazing into each other's eyes. I suppose she would be looking into my blue eyes and thinking how different they looked from hers. I looked into her eyes and I was in another world where there was no time or distance, no hatred or war, no up or down, no ground and no gravity, only she and I. And we would lie there like that for hours.

Once when we were lying there looking at each other she told me that I had beautiful blue eyes. This came as such a shock to me because I never really considered my eyes to be beautiful. I was always so captivated by her brown eyes. When she told me she loved my blue eyes it was at that moment that it dawned on me what exactly the key to all life in the universe is. The key to life is that opposites attract...

...OPPOSITES ATTRACT

Opposites attract. It's elementary science. Negatively charged particles bond with the positively charged particles. This bonding of particles creates mass and mass generates gravity. Gravity holds the atmosphere intact and our feet on the ground. If it were not for positive ions attracting negative ions, every mass form on the planet would simply come apart. The world would come undone.

If the forces of nature were to change abruptly and positive and negative stopped attracting, we would never know it. Our brains would vaporize before the electrical impulses of warning were ever sent. Plainly put, everything would cease to exist if not for the fact that opposites attract.

Opposite forces are what make the world go round. Day gives in to night and night gives in to day. Blinding white light from the sun in day gives way to black nothingness of space at night, until it gives way to the blinding white light from the sun in day, which in time yields to the darkness of night. An on and on it goes. Dark and light, black and white, wrong and right, why must life be a plight?

What is it about 'opposites attract' that has been so hard for the white man to accept throughout time? Rather than accept that which is nature and live in harmony with the rest of God's creatures, the white man has attempted to change or mold the universe into his own liking. The white man worked hard and came up with a device that will split apart this positive/negative energy force when he produced the Atom Bomb.

And the devastating destruction produced by the Atom Bomb was not enough, so the Anglo pushed further to undo the forces of nature until he came up with the Hydrogen Bomb. And still not satisfied, the Anglo now holds in his possession a Nuclear Bomb by which to eradicate wrong from right, negative from positive and black from white in the universe for eternity...

...ETERNITY

Eternity -- that's how long the promise of love is. And it was this eternal love that possessed me to pack up all I owned and run away with Carolyn across the country so that we could be together and away from her parents and my parents who were all opposed to our being together.

Carolyn was eight months pregnant at the time. She had just learned about the pregnancy in its fifth month. When I learned she was pregnant, I went through a period of panic and denial. All of a sudden and just like that I was going to be a daddy. I'm not sure if it was the sudden weight of responsibility or the sudden knowledge of commitment that hit me so hard, but whatever it was I panicked.

I always knew that I loved Carolyn and that I wanted her to be my wife one day, but when the day was suddenly upon me by virtue of a baby whether I was ready or not, I did the same thing any good, decent, self-respecting man would do in my position. I ran.

I packed my bags and took off for New Orleans to live with my uncle and aunt. I was a very confused puppy. I knew I loved Carolyn, but how could I be sure it was love forever? I didn't know what love was. I had never had such strong emotions for anyone else in my life, not even close and I knew that to be true, but how could I be sure? I wanted to know if what I was feeling was love, or lust? As I said before, I wasn't exactly the lady killer in high school. Some guys had all the girls chasing them, but definitely not me.

I had to know, had to be sure. I was determined to give someone else a try. Before I committed to a relationship that was different for the times, I wanted to be sure that I knew what I was doing. So I took off for New Orleans leaving six month pregnant Carolyn behind.

I spent the next six weeks living at my aunt and uncle's house and working at a downtown New Orleans bank at night and sleeping during the day and hooking up with this girl I had met down there. I would check us into a motel room and we would spend the weekend having sex. Nice sex. This girl was quite beautiful and exciting to be with, but truth was the whole while I just couldn't get Carolyn out of my mind. I found myself comparing everything this girl did to Carolyn. As the weeks in New Orleans went by I began missing Carolyn more and more and it became clear to me that I just had to be with her.

So I began calling her long distance to talk. I had changed jobs by then and was now working at a shipyard in Avondale, La, and I would spend my lunch time on the pay phone dropping in coin after coin to keep talking to her.

Then I took a weekend and flew back home to see her. My mother picked me up from the airport and as we drove the hour back home I told her that I was going to marry Carolyn. I expected her to blow up or wreck the car or something, but she simply asked me if I was sure that is what I wanted to do, and when I said yes she simply sighed and didn't say another word about it.

And boy was it was great to see Carolyn again. We spent the two days I was there planning a wedding. The plan was for me to go back to New Orleans and get my stuff then drive back to Virginia to get married. I was excited at first about the wedding, and Carolyn was excited as well, but the main reason we were doing it was because her father had demanded it. He did not want his daughter to have a baby, especially a white man's baby, unless the white man had committed to her. So I was going to do what he demanded and what I knew to be the right thing and get married. I knew I wanted it anyway.

So the weekend was a whirlwind of talking and squeezing and then I flew back to New Orleans and once I got there and thought things through some more I once again got cold feet. I called Carolyn and we talked about it and I asked her to run away with me. I told her I knew I did want to get married to her one day but that I couldn't see going through all this with her baby bump sticking out of her wedding dress just to appease her father. The poor girl, I knew she was miserable being pregnant and living with her parents and especially her dad who let her know every day how disappointed he was with her.

The night before I flew back to Orleans I had slipped a couple of one-hundred dollar bills into a small compartment in Carolyn's pocketbook unbeknownst to her. I guess maybe I knew that I wasn't sure about the wedding from the start and I wasn't sure if I could go on with it, so I wanted Carolyn to have some money in case she needed to get away from her father and if not, then the money would go towards the baby's needs. I told Carolyn where the money was in her purse and to use it to get to New Orleans as quickly as she could and we would head west. So that's what she did. She packed a suitcase and got a friend to take her to the bus station while her parents were at work and she came to New Orleans.

The day she arrived I had packed all my belongings into my car after my aunt and uncle had gone to work. I hadn't told them I was leaving because I didn't want to listen to them try to talk me out of it, or have them call my mom and have her get on me. I think my aunt and uncle suspected something was up with me, but they probably weren't sure what I was going to do and they never said anything to me. But they saw that I was spending a lot of time on the telephone back in my little room they provided for me.

I drove down to the bus station and picked Carolyn up. There she was all seven months pregnant and she still looked like a beautiful angel. Her back ached after a grueling two day bus ride to get there and after a good night's rest on a nice bed in a motel we set off together cross country unsure of where we were going we just headed west.

I made a makeshift bed of clothes in the backseat of my small car so that Carolyn could lie down for most of the journey. She clambered into the back seat and lay down then smiled a big smile up at me as if to say this will work just fine, and I beamed with happiness as I climbed behind the wheel of the spacecraft that would carry us to our Shangri-La.

Houston, Texas was our first stop. I had been welding at the shipyard in New Orleans, so I though maybe I could get on at a shipyard in Houston. We drove around checking out the shipyards, but the barrios around them were so filthy and run down and impoverished that it left a bad impression on me and I did not want to live there, so we kept on going and our next stop was San Diego, California.

We drove west and then crested a mountain and looked down onto the setting sun over the seaside community that was San Diego. What a magnificent sight to behold it was. The valley was a menagerie of structures and long shadows and rolling hillsides with lights twinkling in the dusk. The city rose up in the distance and the skyline was a flaming huge orange ball slowly sinking below the horizon. I had a good feeling about this place. It knew it was going to be our new home.

We checked into a motel and the next day I went looking for a job...

...A JOB

When you are a convicted felon, no one wants to give you a job. Nobody wants to give you a chance. No one wants to hire a criminal. Why should they hire a criminal when there are too many others out there looking for work?

Being unemployed with two sons to feed, I was forced to go on welfare. Being on welfare was the pits. Using food stamps at the grocery store was even worst. I had been at the grocery store many times in my life and saw people pay for their food with stamps. I had always found myself studying those people and wondering why they didn't have real money to pay for their food with. Though I had always been sympathetic towards those in poverty, watching someone pay for their groceries with food stamps when I had to pay seventy-five or one hundred dollars cash for mine was always a bit disconcerting to me. Especially when it seemed that everyone who used food stamps to buy food always had cash to pay for their carton of cigarettes and case of beer.

Demoralizing, humiliating, and just down right embarrassing is what it was. I would mill about with my full cart near the front of the store waiting for the checkout lines to clear so that no one else would be in line and see me paying with food stamps. When someone got in line behind me (as always seemed to be the case) I could never look at them. I would keep my head down and my baseball cap pulled down low on my forehead. I would keep the stamps hidden away in my pocket until the last possible moment when I would have to present them to the cashier. Perhaps it was just my imagination but it seemed that the cashiers would even frown when I handed them the stamps.

I became so humiliated using the food stamps that I began doing my grocery shopping late at night around midnight. This helped some, but the problem with that was that there was usually only one cashier at that late hour and a long line of people with one or two items would sometimes congregate behind me while I was checking out and so now there was an audience watching me pay with food stamps. It was a no-win situation, but at least we weren't starving and this was the purpose of the stamps so I couldn't complain about them at all. I didn't have a job so I didn't have a choice.

So there I was, an unemployed father of two children and convicted child molester to boot, pushing a grocery cart around the supermarket after midnight with food stamps in his pocket. I must admit it was an all-time low for me. Once I ran into a guy named Ron that I used to work with. I liked Ron a lot. Ron had a deformed arm and hand from birth that was smaller than normal but he didn't let that bother him at all and I really admired him for that. Ron was a real jokester and all round great guy in my book! And I saw Ron there in the aisle at the store and I spoke to him and he looked up and saw me and a big frown crossed his face and he asked me tersely what do you want? I was crushed. He just stood there looking at me with this disgusted look on his face and I just turned and walked away. It crushed me.

Things did not look very bright for me but I had to keep on trying...

...TRYING

I'm still trying to find a job. I had an interview last Monday morning and I think it went pretty well. The interview was for a computer technician job in the town's administrative offices. The pay isn't the best, but it is a job. I was interviewed by two women close to my age. They were very nice and I felt the interview went well.

The job involves working with a "medium frame" computer, the AS400, a mid-sized computer perfect for a small to medium sized business. I have lots of experience working with computers of all different sizes and once worked at a bank which had a system very similar to this one.

And I feel I had all the right answers for the ladies, and they took lots of notes, and I had on my suit and tie and I was looking sharp. And the interview, or interrogation if you will, went very smoothly and I felt I was really bonding with the two nice ladies until the interview was over and one of the ladies handed me back my application form I had filled out and said that I had neglected to fill out one section of it. The section I had left blank was the Criminal Record section where the question is always the same:

Have you ever been convicted of a felony? If so, explain.___________

____

____

____

____

And I took the form feeling very stupid and humiliated, and I knew that I had purposely left it blank in hopes that they wouldn't ask, but of course they did. And I just hadn't been sure what to put down there, because if I put that I am a convicted felon will I get an interview at all. And if I put no, I do not have a felony conviction, what if they hire me then run a criminal background check and find I am a convicted felon and then fire me. I just didn't know what to put down so I left it blank in hopes it wouldn't come up. Wrong.

I took the form from the lady's hand and placed it purposefully in front of me and picked up a pen lying there on the table and then sat there for a moment looking down at the form. I was conscious of two sets of eyes burning a hole in the top of my head. I thought for a moment that I might just lie and check the 'NO' box indicating that I had no criminal record, but I somehow I felt the ladies knew of my conviction and I was afraid to check no. Call it paranoia, but I just felt as if they knew. Just as I felt as I walked down the street and whenever I made eye contact with someone I felt that they were looking at me because they knew.

So I checked the box 'YES', I have a criminal conviction, and as I began writing I began talking and I looked up at the ladies and into their eyes and began a brief, albeit comprehensive, explanation of my arrest and subsequent conviction and all the while as I talked the ladies listened attentively to my confessional with compassionate expressions and every now and then their eyes would soften as if to say "Oh you poor man." After I finished talking the ladies remained silent as I completed filling out the *Criminal Record* section of the application.

As I stood to leave I asked if my felony conviction would completely rule me out for the job and they quickly assured me that it would not. They had such nice smiles that I felt they were really telling me the truth. They said they would be completing their interviews in the next few days and would have their decision by the end of the week and would call me if I was the one.

Two weeks later and still no call...

...CALL

Child Enforcement Services gave me a call to find out if my youngest son was still living with me. It seems that my ex-wife called them and claimed that he was living in Florida with his grandmother, my mom. He had been to visit her for a few weeks over the summer, but he was now back living with me and in school. I was taken aback at the claim and as our conversation progressed my feelings of amused disbelief gave way to a bit of anger and then the lady took on a defensive air and that angered me even more.

The conversation began by her asking me if Landon was living in Florida. I said no, he was living with me and was going to the local high school, the only high school in town. She said she would have to have conformation of this from the school.

I asked her why this conversation was even taking place. She said that my ex-wife, who was having a paycheck garnished each week for a measly $50 in child support, had come to their offices and claimed that my son no longer lived with me. She wanted to terminate the amount that was being taken from her check every week in child support.

It perturbed me that my ex-wife had done this. She knew he didn't live in Florida. But then again, maybe she didn't know. She never saw him, never called him, and never did anything for him except to have $50 per week taken from her paycheck against her will, so maybe she honestly didn't know where he was.

Regardless, she could have simply picked up the phone and made a phone call to find out if her own child still lived an hour down the road from her. There was no reason for her to go to Social Services and make such an absurd claim. No reason at all, except to try to make things more difficult for me.

I suggested to the lady on the other end of the line that she simply call the high school here in town and get the confirmation that the boy was enrolled there, or request them to send confirmation to her. I wasn't busy at the time mind you considering I wasn't working, and I could have done it myself, but I figured that one state agency talking to another would clear the matter up more pronto then I could.

However, the lady told me she could not contact the school herself and request that information. She said it would have to be requested by me, the father.

Then I got pissed. I was already in a foul mood anyway, so this just pushed me to the boiling point. I didn't understand why I was being placed at this inconvenience to go out of my way to do something it seemed to me she was being paid to do. And wasn't I doing enough already? I was the one caring for the boy. My ex-wife was contributing less than $200 a month (correction- the money was being deducted from her paycheck before she ever got her hands on it) towards the child's well-being and that was the extent of her obligation and that was the extent of her effort as well - nothing more.

I gave the lady from the Enforcement Services an ear-full about being a single parent with a future that looks bleak, and all the while I heard her typing just as fast as her fingers could carry her and I am sure she was taking all my diatribe down to use against me at some later date. I could tell from her comments and tone that she was completely unsympathetic towards my plight and was undoubtedly on the side of my ex-wife – because after all I was a child molester.

I told her how I had been thinking of late of how life might be easier if I didn't have the "burden" of children, and I apologized for using the word burden in the same sentence with my children and that burden was a terrible word to choose, but accurate one none-the-less. And I told the lady that it sure would be nice to get some sort of help from the mother every now and then, like a little free time away from the kids or some new clothes or shoes or school supplies or something -- anything.

I went on to explain that my ex-wife must be up to something because she could have simply picked up the phone and called here to find out if her son was still living less than an hour away from her, the same as she could have since the day she walked out on us. Or she could have called someone she knows who has children in school and asked if they had seen her son. There were ways for her to find out.

All the while this woman was steady pounding on her keyboard as I went on about how the ex-wife had cursed out our oldest boy out when he called her because of some mounting problems (mostly financial) and after cursing him out for having to audacity to call her to ask her for money she told him to never call her again. The lady had stopped typing now and was silent.

I said if I had the opportunity to bail out of parenthood for a penalty of $200 a month that I would take the penalty but that I would then be accused of child abandonment while my ex-wife was getting off scott free.

The woman on the other end then spat back at me to contact the school and have them mail her the information and that would be the end of it.

I commented that it sure was a shame that by playing games my ex-wife was putting extra work on me and extra work on the Child Support Enforcement case worker, and lady on the other end was typing away again. I told her I felt she was taking sides with my ex-wife who I am sure came into her office smartly dressed in a business suit and crying her eyes out over the monster who would not allow her to see her children. And then I said my ex was up for best-actress at the Academy Awards for Crack Addicts and the lady really got hot then and told me that she felt sorry for the children and that she didn't care about me or their mother, only the children.

And I would love to have been a fly on the wall to see what the woman was typing as I went on about how fucked up it had been for years with the mother not doing one damn thing for the kids and I am sure that the woman was quickly typing stuff like '...father is easily irritated' and '...father sounds capable of violence' and '... father is a rambling idiot.'

And it didn't feel good either to know that I, the one taking the responsibility of raising the boys, was no better than the abandoning parent who hadn't so much as said "boo" to her children in years.

And it made me wonder why I even try sometimes. All these state agencies are full of women who side with each other. It is an underground network. It is the reason you never see a woman go to the bathroom by herself. They always like to go together so they can plot and scheme to take over the world.

The term "deadbeat dad" is one their most favorites to harp on, but find one who is not a deadbeat and who is doing the right thing and taking care of his children and what do they say -- "That's the son-of-a-bitch who ran his wife off."

And I wondered why try. And then I wondered if the lady from the Support Enforcement Services knew that I am a convicted child molester, and then I knew that the lady knew because of course she knew, my ex-wife had come in to talk to her and there is no doubt that she would have told her. So always I lose.

I know I was a little sharp with the lady and shouldn't have been but it just pissed me off because it has all gone against me every time and me the one doing the right thing, the only thing, the that I must do as a parent responsible for bringing these children into the world yet I am constantly the bad guy and monster the whole while and my wife is but a poor poor victim. Jeez, when will these people see the light...

...LIGHT

A light bulb went out in my apartment yesterday. It was one of those expensive light bulbs that are guaranteed to last for five years. 'The Titanium Bulb, guaranteed to last you five years or we will replace it free of charge. I remembered vividly the sales pitch. I paid many times more for it than I would a standard light bulb, but the guarantee hooked me so I went for it. The bulb had lasted about six months.

I had purchased the bulb from a television advertisement, and after the package had arrived in the mail I made sure to place my receipt in the empty box and stored it in the closet. I went to my closet and retrieved the box. I looked inside and, sure enough, the receipt was there; much to my elation. This was an expensive bulb you know, Titanium, and being the thrifty son of a bitch that I am, I wanted to get my money's worth out of it. I looked at the date to verify the purchase date and I saw that I had gotten the bulb a full eleven months ago. It amazed me how time flew anymore. Despite my lapse in time, the warranty on the bulb was still active. Therefore, they owed me a new bulb.

My next question was who was they? I looked on the box and found a toll free number to call. It was not easy to locate the number on the box that was covered by 'The Titanium Bulb, guaranteed to last you five years or we will replace it free of charge' in big bold letters in neon, but I found the number and called it.

"Acme Bulb Company, home of The Titanium Bulb, guaranteed to last you five years or we will replace it free of charge. How may I direct your call please?"

"I have a Titanium Bulb that I purchased almost a year ago that has burned out. I would like to know how to get it replaced for free please."

"Sir, our bulbs last five years. How long ago did you purchase your bulb?" was her response.

"I bought it back in October of last year. It only lasted me eleven months!"

"That is impossible, sir. Our bulbs last five years," she deadpanned back.

"Five years or five hundred years, I don't care, this bulb only lasted eleven months. Not even *one* year! Now I would like it to be replaced like your guarantee says."

"Are you sure it is one of our bulbs sir? Can you look on the bulb and see the words Titanium Bulb on the top of it?"

I studied the bulb and could vaguely make out the lettering, and sure enough it said Titanium Bulb. "Yes, it does say Titanium Bulb on it. I'm sure it is one of your bulbs because I ordered it myself and put it in myself. It is a Titanium Bulb and it only lasted one year. Not even."

"There must be some mistake sir. Our bulbs last five years. Guaranteed. Are you sure that is the same bulb that you put in? Could someone have come in and replaced the Titanium Bulb you put in with a different Titanium Bulb that was much older? Can you be sure that is the same bulb you put in? I don't mean to sound suspicious about all this sir, but you see this is all so perplexing because our bulbs last five years. Can you be sure that is the same bulb?"

I was getting a little peeved at this point. I just wanted them to send me a new bulb, and I didn't appreciate being reproached. Raising my voice a bit, I replied, "*What the hell is this?* I bought your bulb because of the guarantee. I paid a hell of a lot of money for this bulb, because of the guarantee. Now you are questioning me to try to get out of the guarantee? What the hell is this*? Of course it's the same bulb I put in a year ago!* Not even a year ago."

"There's no reason to raise your voice with me sir," she replied, I am just trying to establish a few facts here sir. And one fact is that you are mistaken about paying a lot of money for the guarantee on our bulbs. You did not pay a dime for the guarantee on our bulbs. We offer our guarantee free of charge to you, the consumer. The fact is that you paid a lot of money for the bulb, not the guarantee. You paid a lot of money for the bulb that is a Titanium Bulb, the highest quality light bulb on the market today, manufactured with Titanium alloys and hermetically sealed and individually tested by a team of experts. The price you paid was for the bulb sir, not the guarantee."

There was a brief pause as if she were waiting for me to reply or acknowledge what she just said, and just as I was about to explode in her ear, she went on. "These are expensive bulbs sir, and in great demand around the country and the world even. Do you live in an apartment or do you own your home sir?

"I live in an apartment. What does that have to do with anything?"

"Well there you go, sir. You live in an apartment. Maintenance people are probably in and out all the time there, isn't that true, sir?"

"Well,..."

"Of course it's true, sir. We have had instances in the past where maintenance people have gone into apartments and swapped out new Titanium Bulbs with older Titanium Bulbs. Our bulbs are valuable pieces of property, sir, and in high demand. We suspect there may be an organized entity that is going around swapping out our bulbs. Can you be sure that the bulb you have in front of you is the very same bulb you replaced only a year ago?"

This was so ridiculous that my anger was turning to disbelief, and I almost started laughing at the woman. Of course I couldn't prove that this was the same bulb. All bulbs looked the same to me. "Yes I am sure that it is the same bulb. I When I put the bulb in, I placed an 'x' on it with a permanent marker so that I could identify it just in case someone came in and stole it. I had heard of the suspected crime ring that was targeting Titanium light bulbs, so I took precautions," I lied as I wrote an 'x' on the bulb with a permanent marker.

The woman was silent for a moment, then said "Are you sure that is your 'x'? These crooks are clever you know."

"Just tell me what I need to do to get my free replacement!" I screamed. *"This is absolutely preposterous!* I call you for a new bulb and you question me like I am an idiot or a criminal. Let speak to your supervisor. Yes, I want to speak to your supervisor right now. I have never been treated with such disrespect before in my life. What kind of company is this? Let me speak to your supervisor right now."

"There is no reason to get all huffy sir. I am only doing my job. I'm sorry if you take offense to my questions, but this is only standard procedure and my supervisor would only verify this for you. It is my duty to establish the facts, and that is what I am trying to do here, sir. I only have one more question and then we can get a new bulb out to you ASAP. Now, can we continue sir or do I have to go locate my supervisor?"

"Alright, alright, we can go on. What is your last question so that I can get on with my life and you can send me a new bulb. I'd rather get my money back at this point. Is that possible that I can just get my damn money back and be done with you and your company and your sorry Titanium Bulbs?"

"There is no reason to slander our product, sir. We offer the most durable, highest-tech, longest lasting light bulb on the market today. If you are sure your bulb did not last five years, then there must be a reason for it burning out. No, we cannot refund your money. That is not a part of our guarantee. Our guarantee states that we will replace your bulb for free, not refund your money. Now, my last question for you is do you recall experiencing any power fluxes in the past twelve months, fluxes that may have caused your lights to flicker or your appliances to cut off? A power flux could cause the element in our bulbs to burn out, and I'm afraid our guarantee does not cover product failure due to a power flux."

"Never. We have never have power fluxes here for as long as I have been living here and that is almost ten years," I lied again.

"I find that hard to believe, sir. I have lived in many apartment complexes and they always have power fluxes. I'm not calling you a liar sir, but I find it hard to believe that you haven't had any power fluxes. Do you recall ever experiencing your lights growing brighter for a second, or perhaps flickering during a storm? Have you ever had a storm there, sir?"

"Never. The weather here is perfect. The sun always shines and the air never stirs above a slight breeze. In fact, our weather is so perfect here that scientists are studying this region to find why it is so perfect. Now send me my new bulb please."

"Ok sir. No storms, no power fluxes, no crime. Are you in heaven? I mean come on sir, those conditions only exist in heaven. You're calling from Heaven, aren't you?"

"Yes, I am in heaven," I replied.

"I'm sorry sir, we don't ship there."

"JUST SEND ME A GODDAMNED BULB like your guarantee says please!" I screamed.

"Ok, ok sir. No need to get so testy. I was just kidding. Can't you take a little joke sir?"

"No I can't. Now what do you need from me to send me a new bulb? You need my address don't you?"

"No sir. You will need to send the burned out bulb back to us in its original container along with a copy of your receipt and a note explaining what happened to the Titanium Bulb to cause it to burn out before five years. Be sure to provide your return address. Once we receive the bulb, we will ship you out a new one."

"What? I have to send you back the old bulb? Why?"

"Oh come on, sir. We can't just send out these expensive Titanium Bulbs to anyone who calls and says they want one. We would be out of business in a heartbeat. Why, the organized criminals would have a field day if we did not require proof-of-purchase and you know that."

"But if I have to send you back the burned out bulb it is going to cost me money on top of the goodly amount I already paid for the bulb. Your guarantee states that you replace the bulb for free. Or do I send it C.O.D. and you pick up the shipping costs?"

"No sir. We don't pick up the shipping costs. We will send you out a new bulb free of charge just as our guarantee states once we receive the old bulb. Our guarantee says nothing about covering shipping."

"Well I'll be damned. This is the damndest thing I have ever heard of. It is going to cost me more money now just to get a new bulb for free. This is a racket, that's what it is. A racket! You guys are a bunch of crooks."

"Watch it, sir. All of our calls are taped. I would watch what I said if I were you. We are a respectable company selling the best light bulb on the market. We don't take kindly to slander."

"Whatever. I'm going to send you the bulb and I expect a new one right away. No tricks, no funny business. Just send me my bulb."

"Send us everything I asked for and we will do this. It is our guarantee. One thing I might point out sir is to be sure to package your bulb properly and pad it so that it does not break during shipping. If we receive the bulb broken we will not replace it. We do not guarantee broken bulbs."

"Can you tell me how in the hell I can be sure it will get to you in one piece please!?!"

"Why of course sir," she said, "just sent it via guaranteed mail."

"Perfect..."

...PERFECT

In the beginning Carolyn was the most perfect wife and mother in the whole wide world. We started out as a family in San Diego, California. When we got to San Diego Carolyn was eight months pregnant. I sold my car and we used some of the money to get an apartment in La Mesa, a suburb of San Diego, some went for Carolyn to get a check-up at the baby doctors, and the rest went for groceries and furniture rental and phone hook-up and stuff like that. It didn't take long for our money to just disappear. We were literally flying by the seat of our pants but we didn't care because we were together at last and nothing else mattered.

Despite the instability, Carolyn was a rock. She was strong, intelligent, and blessed with a statuesque build and disarming good looks. She was the most beautiful woman in the world to me. And she could cook with the best of them. And damn was she ever fast in a kitchen. She could whip up a meal in no time. Sometimes I used to think she must have blinked her eyes and made the meal appear, just like Barbara Eden used to do in *I Dream of Genie*. To me she really was remarkable. She did the laundry and grocery shopped and kept our small dwelling clean, and even worked a full time job most of the time we were together to boot.

I was the handy man around the house who put up shelves and fixed things that were broken and built the deck and kept the cars running, and most of the time I kept both a full time and part time job simultaneously. I always felt that I had it the toughest because of the two jobs, but once I became a single parent I learned that I had it easy compared to what Carolyn did on a daily basis. Yet she never complained and merely went about every task as if it was a walk in the park. She seemed to have unlimited energy, and I admired her for it so.

I luckily found a job pumping gasoline at a filling station which was only a ten minute walk from our apartment. I worked there everyday for weeks until I got on with a carpenter who needed a helper and paid better. He lived not too far from the apartment complex where Carolyn and I lived, and he would swing by and pick me up for work every morning. He was a really super fellow and I can tell you he was a real Godsend for us in those early days. I was even able to stay on at the filling station part-time a few nights a week, so our finances looked better and it began to look like we just might be ok. Then we just waited for our first child to be born.

We did not have to wait long. I had just started the construction job when the site foreman drove up to where I was hammering on a roof and told me that my wife had called to say she was on her way to the hospital. My boss rushed me to the hospital in his old Chrysler with the push button transmission on the dashboard, and when I got there Carolyn was in a post-natal delivery room holding our first born to her breast. He was so tiny up against her, and it warmed my heart to see them both there doing just fine. I got to hold him for a brief moment, but I had never ever held a baby before and he seemed so fragile to me that I handed him right back to Carolyn. She was totally at ease with him.

The doctor who delivered him was there too and I thanked him sincerely. He said that he didn't have to do anything because it was one of the easiest deliveries he had ever handled. He said he arrived in the delivery room just in the nick of time to catch the little fellow as he literally popped out. Carolyn was in labor for less than an hour and it was all one easy delivery, easy being a relative term of course. It didn't surprise me because she was a model of efficiency in everything she did, so why should this be anything different. It was a sign of her strength, and it was one of the things I admired and loved in her.

It was a pretty neat feeling there that day in that hospital room. I was now a dad. Perhaps it was that old thing of proof or confirmation or, ah, affirmation, of one's manhood, and although I never was one for jutting out the old chest (what I had of one) and strutting around, all I know is that I felt pretty neat there that day. And my son was so perfect looking and his skin was so smooth and soft and not wrinkly at all like I had always thought newborns to be, and he had ten little fingers and ten little toes that Carolyn would count over and over.

And I was one proud papa and Carolyn was glowing like an angel and I couldn't have been happier.

And that is how it was in the beginning of the world...

...THE BEGINNING OF THE WORLD

And the Earth's temperature changed so suddenly
that the forests caught fire at once
and just from an ever-so-slight variation
in her elliptical path around her sun
the planet earth began to bake...

...and in but a few hours time
her core was melting
and volcanoes spewed forth lava and ash
and new volcanoes burst upward with fury
as the Earth became a molten ball...

...and all that was ground melted and sank
and all that was concrete sizzled to paste
and all that was steel oozed and bubbled
and all that was green turned black and red..

...and all that was nuclear imploded and dissolved
and all that was ocean boiled away to steam
and all that was flesh disintegrated...

...as the Earth began anew...

...ANEW

After only a year in California we moved back home to Virginia and started anew. We were married now. It had been a mere formality for us, but a big deal to Carolyn's father who had insisted we get married before he would accept us. I guess this was the final proof for him that I truly loved his daughter, as well as a contractual agreement to care for her and any offspring resulting from our union. Carolyn's daddy was no dummy – far from it. We got married in a small chapel in a small town outside of San Diego named Chula Vista. There was a priest and an organ player who doubled as the witness, and Carolyn and me. The ceremony was very simple and the vows we uttered were from an Indian wedding ceremony. I should have seen the writing on the wall right then because, just as an Indian giver, she gave her love to me then took it back.

But alas, I did not see the writing on the wall, all I saw through my tears of happiness was my beautiful wife and her beautiful, loving eyes and an eternity of happiness ahead. Our honeymoon was a night to ourselves in our apartment, a real treat to anyone with a newborn. My carpenter boss and his wife and family babysat our son to allow us the time together. As humble as it all was, it was a special day for me indeed that I can only look back upon with bitter sweetness.

So we came back home to begin anew as a family. Things went well. All of our friends and family welcomed us back with open arms, and everyone just adored the baby. Some say that mixed children are the most beautiful children in the world, and I can't say that I disagree, but all babies are beautiful regardless of color or race. But so many people just loved that little fellow of ours with his big smile and puffy round cheeks. Everyone just loved to pinch his cheeks because they were so big. He was a hefty baby, not fat, just stout, and grew to be a solid, healthy boy. People in grocery stores and the shopping malls and everywhere just loved to ogle over him, even those who probably didn't like the fact that me and Carolyn were a mixed couple but couldn't resist the charm of an innocent mixed baby.

Everyone accepted us as we were and life was good back home here. We both got jobs at the local university and, though neither of us made a lot of money, we always pooled out money together and worked as a team to get by. Carolyn was an incredible person. To me she was superwoman. She could cook and she kept a clean home and she knew all about raising children as she had helped raise her younger brothers growing up. She was so fast in the kitchen and when dinner was served it was always hot and delicious and right on time.

While Carolyn kept up the home I kept the vehicles running and worked two jobs to make ends meet. The entire time we were together I can't remember not working two jobs, one a full time and one a part time. I would leave from one job and go directly to the other to work another two or three hours and not get home till late evening every day. Looking back perhaps I spent too much time away from home. I wasn't the type to go out all the time with my buddies leaving my wife behind to care for the kids on her own. I say kids because six years after our first son was born we had a second son. I did go out on occasion with the guys to have a drink or to play golf, and once a year I would take a road trip with my buddies to Atlanta to see a few Brave's games, but otherwise I stayed at home. I liked being at home. I liked being around my wife and my kids. Where to the rest of the world I felt as if I didn't fit in, as if I were from another world, an alien, at home I was at peace with my family. Looking back perhaps I spent too much time *at* home.

Looking back I don't have a clue what the hell happened.

I just don't know where things went wrong. Life seemed good. After our second son came along we once again got the oohhhhs and aahhhhs from people out and about in the stores. I am biased but both my boys were such beautiful babies. I know all parents feel this. And they are. This boy was not the chubby baby that our first one was. This boy was much thinner, and a bit lighter in complexion as well, and every bit the cutie that the first one was. People just loved our children. Why couldn't they be that nice to us as well?

But anyway, all was good and I was happy and I thought Carolyn was happy and we worked and played and set our sites on moving into a new home, a real home, and we went to the bank to see if we qualified for a house and we found out that we couldn't because of some bad credit history on Carolyn's part and I recall that it seemed to bother her more then it bothered me and it wasn't too long after that that Carolyn seemed to go into a bout of slight depression. Our youngest was only a couple of years old and our oldest was eight and I don't know if Carolyn suddenly felt like she was trapped in poverty in a mobile home with kids and diapers and no way out, or if it was some delayed form of postpartum depression but she seemed to go through a period where all she wanted to do was sleep on the couch in the evening after dinner and I became concerned and I encouraged her to get together with some girlfriends and go out and have some fun.

During our marriage I had always done other things now and then with my friends, but Carolyn had spent little time out with others. When she began to seem a little depressed I confronted her with it and told her I felt she just needed a little break. Heck, we all need a little break sometimes from the weighty responsibilities of kids and house and spouse and work and you name it. I told her that she went about everything like the cooking and doing the wash and cleaning the house at full speed and she needed to try slowing down a little or she would burn out.

Thinking back, I remember reading Toni Morrison's *The Bluest Eye* where she spoke with disdain in her voice of the slender, dark-skinned girls who looked so proper and stood so erect in church and who picked up behind you even before you had gotten up to leave during a visit. I never quite understood Ms. Morrison's disdain for these dark skinned girls, but I remember reading this and recalling how Carolyn used to be so efficient and so tireless at keeping our home clean, and she would begin straightening up even before or immediately after company would leave and I wondered what Morrison was trying to say.

Was she trying to say that the slender, dark skinned girls were born to be maids, or servants, because of their dark skin? I always noticed how lighter skinned blacks always seemed to look down on darker skinned blacks as if they were inferior, so was Morrison making reference to this?

Was Morrison perhaps commenting on how the darker skinned, slender black girls behaved like machines, programmed by a heritage of and endless life of servitude, victims of their past and present and future? Carolyn was like a machine. Did she feel victimized as well?

Or did Morrison feel disdain because she was jealous of the dark, slender black girls who looked so proper and stood so erect in their Sunday best and who's hearts were so strong and who's bodies were so capable and efficient and able to bear strong healthy children. Was Morrison's disdain simply based on a woman's jealousy of another? I can't be sure, just as I couldn't be sure of what was happening to Carolyn. I just didn't know.

So we talked about her lack of energy and motivation she said she did not know why she was feeling the way she did but it was nothing to be alarmed about. She wrote it off as being low iron count or allergies or a cold that was making her feel a little run down. Poor girl worked full time and then came home and took care of the house and kids. Once I began doing it for myself I quickly realized that it will drive a person crazy. If only I had seen it back then.

Carolyn agreed that an occasional break might do her some good, so she began going out occasionally with her sister and some friends. I was more than happy to stay at home and watch over the kids. It was a break for me as well, some space to myself, although I admit that I was most happy when with her by my side. But I would kiss her good bye and tell her to have a good time and she would go out to spend an evening with her girlfriends having a drink and talking gossip or playing Pictionary, the latest game craze.

Little did I know that the reason she had begun going out more frequently was because she had become hooked on crack cocaine. I knew about the crack cocaine epidemic going on around the country in the big cities like New York and Chicago and Miami from reading about it in Time Magazine and seeing it on the national news and I saw how it was devastating black families and communities everywhere but no way did I ever think it was in our small town. But it was, and Carolyn had tried it and had become instantly hooked and the Carolyn I knew and had married was suddenly gone and life as I knew it was now gone forever thanks to the crackle from a little pipe where everyone lost...

...LOST

Another job lost. I had gotten a job at the college after I did not write down my felony conviction on the application form I submitted to them. I lied but it got me the job. I was doing some data entry and programming for them and had been there about six months when my boss came to me and told me that someone in the Personnel Department wanted to see me.

I went next door to Personnel and a lady sat me down and said it had been made known to them that I was a convicted felon and that I had not informed them of that on my application. She apologized but said she had no choice but to let me go, the polite way of saying "you're fired."

To this day I believe that it was my ex-wife who tipped them off just to be hateful, just like the time someone complained to the local Social Services Department that I was an unfit father because my youngest son was seen riding his bicycle in the street.

Social Services came by my apartment one evening to inform me they were going to do a 'home study' on me. I asked why and they said someone had informed them that I wasn't watching my children properly. I was flabbergasted. I asked who called them but they wouldn't tell me who it was. It amazed me that my wife was running around smoking crack and doing absolutely nothing for her children while I had all the burden of responsibility, and now Social Services was there to make things just a little more difficult.

The home study was conducted. It consisted of a few visits from a case worker who inspected my apartment and interviewed me and the children separately. The study concluded I was dong a fine job. They never would tell me who prompted the whole process to begin with, but I am certain it was my estranged wife, just as I am certain it was she who informed the college of my felony conviction.

After the college let me go because I had given false information on my application, I appealed their decision and they allowed me to come back to work because they had been pleased with my work before I was terminated. This was all fine and good, but my position, or stature, in the office was never the same after that. My co-workers treated me differently and, although they were still nice to me, I knew they saw me in a different light now.

My job there lasted about another full year and then I was laid off for "lack of funds" despite the fact I had done some very good things for them including writing a computer program that turned a four-hour long process of ordering supplies for their Central Stores Warehouse, a process that involved multi-part forms and lots of typing, into a process done on a computer that took less than an hour.

Regardless, I was once again facing going back on welfare. But I was determined to stay off of it this time. It is not that I felt that strongly against welfare because I knew it had its purpose in society and had even helped me out in the past in an emergency, but I didn't believe that an able bodied person should get hand outs when they could work for what they needed. And I knew I was able bodied and of sound mind and I felt there was no reason I should be living off of charity.

Since the time I was a young boy I had always had this dream of owning my own snowball stand, just like the ones I used to see everywhere in New Orleans. I had never tasted anything like the snowballs we got whenever we were visiting relatives there, and I knew that they would be a hit back home in Virginia if anyone were to ever open up a stand. So instead of going over to the welfare office and signing up, I spent the next couple weeks at the library gathering all the information I could about starting a business. I drew up a business plan showing how I could make a sweet profit from the sale of sweet snowballs. When I was growing up we used to have a guy who drove around in a station wagon selling snowballs like that, but that was long ago and there was nowhere in town to get a snowball anymore that I knew of.

I polished up my business plan and took it to the local Chamber of Commerce to have them look it over. The man there, a retired gentleman who volunteered his time to help people just starting out, told me that it was one of the most detailed, comprehensive, well prepared plans he had ever seen. He was impressed by it and told me to give it a go. He gave me some names of bankers to go see for a loan and he wished me good luck.

My next step was the loan. I talked to several banks but was turned down by every one of them. I didn't have any money to invest into the venture myself and the banks were afraid to lend me the entire amount. I didn't need much, but I didn't have a job either.

Finally, after much pleading, I was able to get my father to co-sign for the loan and I was off into the business of making snowballs. But not just snowballs, *shaved-ice* snowballs...

...SHAVED-ICE SNOWBALLS

Thank God for shaved-ice snowballs! Where would I have been without my shaved-ice snowballs?

The college basketball season has begun anew and that means more income for me and the boys again, but mainly me. Not a sufficient income to survive off of, mind you, but a nice supplemental boost. Not sufficient income enough to support my oldest boy while he is in college, but a nice income none-the-less when taking into consideration the time involved. The snowball business has come a long way over the past six or so years that I've been in business. What started out as a peddler cart that I pushed down the streets of downtown Blacksburg has evolved into working large public gatherings such as festivals and sporting events and season-long contracts with local swimming pools. No more pushing the cart downtown, dodging traffic and being the butt of many a laughing college student's jokes.

I had all but given up on downtown Blacksburg as a viable money maker. A parking problem has all but killed any general merchandise shopping that may lure families into the downtown area. The town now consists of mostly bars and specialty clothing shops with an occasional tattoo parlor thrown in here and there. In general, it has become a playground for the large university adjacent to it, a sandbox for the Tech kids to play in.

When going into business, I felt that this college market would be my bread and butter. However, I soon learned that too many college kids are interested in beer flavored snowballs, and I didn't carry that one. I did carry root beer, and there were some customers who would stop by almost daily to get the root beer, or the cherry, or the blue raspberry, but not enough. Business was slow on the street. For the most part I learned college kids are not crazy about snowballs because they just want beer. But younger kids are.

Young kids are crazy about snowballs. And thinking back, I was a young kid as well when the snowballs from New Orleans made such an impression on me. And so young kids became my bread and butter, and wasn't that the damnedest thing because here I can't I can't get a job in America because I am a convicted child molester, yet I can get a peddlers license to sell snowballs to packs of screaming, wild, young hooligans who flock to snowballs like bees do to honey.

And here I have been doing this for six years now and I am simply amazed that no one has challenged the fact that a convicted child molester is allowed to work in an environment where there are so many children. Yes, I am simply amazed and absolutely thankful as well. Not that I have ever given anyone any reason to even challenge me for making any improper advances towards their child because I have not, but it is just that I have been in a position where anyone could have made an accusation and I would have been assumed guilty simply because of where I was. You know it's true.

Sure I gave all this some thought before I ever went into the business. I thought about how crazy I was to jump into the fire, to set myself up to have someone humiliate me if they wanted to. I even feared my estranged wife may try to do something, but the bottom line was that I was bound and determined not to let my unjust conviction prevent me from following my dreams or from doing anything that I wanted to for that matter. I was not going to let it destroy me.

And of course, I always wondered, as I still wonder, who knows about my conviction and who doesn't. I used to wonder if the parents who were with their children in line were there to protect them from me, the molester. I wondered if the children who bought the snowballs from me had been forewarned by their parents to beware of that snowball man, the molester. It used to be on my mind constantly at first when I started out in the business, but as time went on and my snowball business grew in popularity I stopped worrying about what everyone else was thinking and just did my job. I provided a good product at a fair price. My product was so low priced that I couldn't possibly get rich from the sale of one, so my whole existence depended on repeat business. Therefore, I did not cut corners or skimp on the sugar. I sold a sweet snowball at a fair price and my customers loved them and came back for more.

I sold to children, and parents, and grandparents, and anyone and everyone aged in between. I found joy in seeing the faces of my customers light up when they tasted my snowballs. I think I got the most satisfaction when an elderly person bought one and told me they loved them. After one elderly lady took a bite of a spearmint flavored snowball, she looked up at me and with raised eyebrows said she hadn't had a snowball like that since she was a young child spending her summer at Coney Island and I could just see the memories dancing around in her wide eyes and it made me feel good. I know that there limitations to a snowball but I also know the way that this simple, inexpensive treat can help to make someone's day just a little brighter, whether young or old.

I guarantee it. If you're not satisfied, then simply mail in your unused portion for a complete refund.

But seriously, I find it strange that I could be allowed to sell snowballs to children, yet I can't be hired to sit in front of a computer and work. I can't get a job with a cable television company to install cable hookups because who wants to take a chance on sending a convicted child molester out into someone's home to do an install?.

I can't get a job working in an office as an assistant because who wants to hire a convicted child molester when there are one hundred other applicants without convictions. I can't get a job as a teacher because who wants to hire a convicted child molester to teach children? I can't get a job as a bartender because the law prevents convicted felons to work where alcohol is being served.

I can't run for President. I couldn't even run for dog warden because my opponent could use my criminal record against me.

But I can sell snowballs, thank goodness.

Until now, that is. Once anyone reads this book I doubt I will ever be in snowballs again.

But if no one reads the book then my secret is safe. But, what secret? I don't have a secret. As I stated before, keeping my conviction a secret is like saying I did something that I am ashamed of and I hope you don't find out. Keeping it a secret is hiding something and this implies dishonesty. Keeping it a secret means that once it is discovered it is dealt with in the context of distrust, dishonesty, disloyalty, and downright disassociation. Any dispute feebly mustered in defense is quickly dismissed and I am quickly and quietly dispensed of. Darn.

I can't get a job as a pizza delivery boy because people find me disgusting.

But onward and upward my good fellow. If enough people read this book at full price then it won't matter if my snowball gig is up because I will be a successful writer. Are convicted child molesters allowed to write? I hope so.

If not, I'll get the laws changed. But how will I do that? Not by voting because I can't vote. Nope, I can't vote. My right to vote was stripped from me the moment I became a convicted felon. As an American citizen I was guaranteed the right to vote. But my right to vote was revoked.

As an American citizen I was also guaranteed the right to a jury trial by my peers. But that was revoked too...

...REVOKED

And then they revoked my bond. Nine months after my original arrest I was served with a summons to appear in court in order for a date to be set for my trial. I went to court and my court appointed attorney was there. Though I had waived my right to an attorney the judge had assigned a public defender to advise me but could not defend me in court. He essentially could be there but had no voice or say.

The reality of an approaching trial and nothing in the form of a defense for me because the state's prosecutor refused to talk or negotiate with me, I was growing increasingly afraid. At the hearing in the courtroom devoid of any witnesses I asked the judge for more time because I wanted to hire an attorney to defend me.

The prosecuting attorney objected and accused me of playing games with the system and asked the judge to revoke my bond. I had run across this judge a few times already in court dealing with my estranged wife and child care matters. I had petitioned the courts for child support once it was obvious to me that she was not going to offer any financial help with the boys and the judge for the hearings was this same guy. I could read the contempt on his face the first time me a white dude and my wife a black woman had stood in front of him. He was a good ole boy from the country in a very conservative state and he did not like what he saw.

I had filed for child support as a last resort to get some financial help to take care of our boys, ages twelve and seven at the time. I wasn't one for running to the law to help me, but in this case I had to swallow my pride and go after child support. This same judge looked at me over his bifocal glasses which had slid down his nose and he said in a scolding tone, "In my day a man didn't ask for help from a woman!"

I snapped back at him, "I'm not doing this for myself. I'm doing it for my kids." Well, I could tell he didn't like that at all. After that, each visit to court became a nightmare. Though I was the one at home taking care of the children while my estranged wife was out running wild, it took me nearly three years and hearing after hearing to finally get these courts to grant me custody of the boys. Three years. On one occasion during our custody battle Carolyn had filed for custody of the youngest boy but not the oldest.

She had not even had any contact with them for over eight months at that time yet she waltzed into court and this same judge granted her custody of *one* child, thus splitting the children up. But she never took custody of him because she never really wanted custody she only wanted to prolong the battle as long as she could so that she wouldn't have to start paying support. She was no dummy. What was even worst was she had lawyers from the Legal Aid Society working for her, the group of lawyers that work for low income individuals who need legal counsel and I had no one because I couldn't afford one. We could barely afford food much less pay an expensive lawyer. I tried to get help from the Legal Aid Society too but they couldn't help me because they were already helping her. Consequently I had no professional legal help.

But getting back to the hearing to set my trial date, I had asked the judge if the trial could be put off a bit longer because I was in the process of looking for some paid legal counsel. I explained that I had found that I could not get any cooperation from the Commonwealth's Attorney's office because the Commonwealth's Attorney refused to meet with me and I could only meet with his assistant.

The judge glared at me from over his spectacles with a face that was a deep red and with eyes that burned, then he swiveled his head to look at the Commonwealth's Attorney and he asked for a comment.

The Commonwealth's Attorney looked at the judge and said that it had almost been a year already since the alleged crime had taken place and he felt I was trying to jerk the system around by postponing the trial as long as I could.

The judge blurted out, *"a year?!?"* and then looked back towards me and glared over his spectacles.

The Commonwealth's Attorney then requested that my bond be revoked and I be retained by the court bailiff for contempt of court.

The judge nodded in agreement and ordered that my bond be revoked and I be held until my trial. He ordered the bailiff to take possession of me.

I stood there not exactly believing what I had just heard. My bond revoked? For what?? I later learned from my parole officer that the courts NEVER revoke anyone's bond not even for murderers and especially not if you are single parent caring for children at home. NEVER. But they revoked mine.

I looked with disbelief at my muted public defender and he just shrugged.

I was led away for contempt of court because I asked for more time to prepare.

Yes, lock that nigger lover up and throw away the key.

I was in shock as I was escorted from the courtroom by two deputies to a holding chamber and then on to the processing cell to be prepared once again for incarceration in the main section, or "on back" as they called it. I was numb. The deputies told me that I would remain behind bars for about a month until my trial by grand jury. There was no getting out this time because my bond had been revoked.

It was an underhanded move by the prosecutor. He had me now. He hated me. He never would talk to me after I had first been arrested and always said he could not discuss the case with me because I was the defendant and it was against the law for the prosecutor to collaborate with the defendant. It's the way the law is designed so that you can't easily defend yourself and are forced to hire a lawyer instead, for a small a fee.

But he did agree to allow me to speak to his assistant, and this I would do though I found that it was merely a ploy to pacify me and give me false hope. I was unable to reason with the assistant at all. He refused to listen to any explanation I had of what had taken place between me and the girl because I was the defendant.

I pleaded that it was my first offense and that I had never been in trouble with the law before not even a speeding ticket and I told him how this young girl had been getting into local college bars at night because she easily passed for a college student due to her appearance. I told him that I could produce witnesses who had seen her in the bars. I informed him I had heard from a reliable source (specifically a teacher from her school) that the teachers had to keep an eye on her because she had been caught after curfew once in a room of boys during and overnight class bus trip to Williamsburg, Virginia. She said that the girl was 'fast' for her age. The teacher told me she would testify for me in court if she could help me. But none of this made any difference according to the prosecutor's assistant. He claimed that all this was hearsay and that her past was inadmissible as evidence.

I pleaded with him that I was a single parent trying to take care of two kids at home that needed me because their mother had deserted them but this didn't faze him either. I was running out of options.

On my last visit to the prosecutors assistant after pleading for nearly fifteen minutes straight he finally looked up at me from behind his desk where he was writing (he was always writing and doing various 'busy' things during my visits as if to let me know that he was not really paying attention and I was welcome to leave anytime) and said that in order for him to reduce the charges against me he would have to have the girls mother's consent. I asked him would he speak to the girl's mother for me and he said that he would. But after that every time I called him he always claimed that the girl's mother would not agree to reduce the charges and therefore the state would not reduce the charges. Period.

I began to panic. Over all the months that this thing was hanging over my head I guess I never really believed that it could go this far. Even after the preliminary hearing where the case had been sent on to the grand jury I always truly believed that the young girl would 'fess up' and admit to someone that she had lied to me about her age. This I knew would exonerate me, but as I later learned this would not even have been good enough because she was underage and once the charges had been levied against me it was 'me vs. the state,' not 'me vs. the girl.' It was me against the law.

So here it was close to show time and I was essentially no farther along then I had been on day one and I began to panic. How had I allowed this to happen? Why hadn't I just gone along with the program and taken on a court appointed lawyer from the start. Why hadn't I just played the game the way the game was meant to be played?

I even had a moderately wealthy uncle offer to pay for my legal expenses at one point and I had turned him down because of my self-righteous, stubborn, ignorant attitude. Was I so consumed with despair over Carolyn having left me that I did not think straight about the serious charges levied against me? Was I so repulsed by a system I perceived to be slanted and unfair that I became bound and determined to beat it my way? Whatever the reason, I tried it my way and was getting nowhere fast and now reality was beginning to set in.

A few weeks before the hearing, I called an attorney I had spoken to when the charges had originally been brought against me. I had dropped my attorney at my first hearing after I had been arrested and so my mother insisted I meet with an attorney that she had used for her divorce from my dad. Her divorce had been a long and painful divorce process. I recalled this lawyer and my dad's lawyer going back and forth and back and forth for years sucking my mother and my father dry with legal bills. She believed in him; I did not. I reluctantly agreed to go speak with him, for her sake more than for mine.

I recall sitting in his office and telling him what all had transpired while my mom sat there too and listened. After I had finished, this attorney said he could get me off no problem for two thousand dollars. To me that was a large amount of money to have to pay to get cleared of something I was not guilty of in the first place. It seemed like extortion to me.

My mother and I thanked him and told him we would let him know and then we left. I told my mother that I would call him that next day and hire him. The next day I called him and told him I thought two thousand dollars was a ridiculous amount of money to pay for him doing next to nothing to earn it and I declined his services with a "thanks but no thanks."

Then there was a guy I had gone to high school with and who was now a defense attorney so I went to talk to him and he offered to help me for a bargain price of five thousand dollars. I told him "thanks but no thanks" too.

So as the hearing date grew nearer I called both of those lawyers up again in desperation to see if they would take the case now but they both said the same thing – "thanks but no thanks". Ouch.

So there I was in court that day to find out how many days I had left before the trial and in the blink of an eye my bond was revoked and I was back behind bars to sit for weeks until my trial!

I sat in that jail cell and my mind raced. My boys would be home from school soon and I wouldn't be there for them. Custody would be handed over to Carolyn who was living with her crack dealer boyfriend. They had guns there - lots of them. What was I to do? It was like I was being treated as guilty before proven innocent. It seemed judgement had already been passed...

...PASSED

I went back to college after being out for twenty years and passed every course I took except one. I got my Bachelor of Arts degree from Virginia Tech there in Blacksburg in four and a half years. This may not seem like much, but I did it while working part time at one sometimes two jobs, operating the snowball business on the side, and raising the two boys as a single parent full time. It was not easy but I was determined to stay in school this time and get my degree for a number of reasons.

One reason that I was bound and determined to get my college diploma was that I had gone to college twenty years before and never even made it through two weeks because I was so intimidated by the size of the school and the fact that it seemed to me I had lost my name and was now only a number - my social security number. I was a bit intimidated by it all having come from a small high school, but bottom line, I was not up to the task at that time in my life.

Another reason was I wanted to set an example for my boys and show them that college was a good thing. I had spent my entire life griping about how unfair society was because some doors were only open to college graduates. Without a degree I never seemed to advance or get anywhere in life. I knew I was a good worker yet I only seemed to just get stuck with more work as my reward. Meanwhile, the fat cats got fatter. So I wanted to show my boys that college was the way while at the same time learning for my own self how it was that a college degree could make a person's shit stop stinking.

But besides all that, the biggest and main reason I wanted to go back to college was that I couldn't get any decent job that paid any decent wages so by enrolling in school I got the maximum amount of financial aid available because of being a single parent in school and honestly this is what got us through for years. I borrowed as much as I could from the government's guaranteed student loan program and, being that I was a non-traditional type student, I qualified for lots relatively speaking. After I finished school I owed enough money to pay for a house. I did what I had to do.

So I just looked at my college experience as a job and I went to my classes every day and I did my homework and I maintained a sufficient grade point average to stay in and I made it through. I survived the early classes, the lectures, the labs, the pop quizzes, more lectures, and the tests with the multiple choice answers including that nasty 'none of the above'...

...'NONE OF THE ABOVE'

I just took my first test of this new semester and I'll be darned if old 'NONE OF THE ABOVE' wasn't there again. God how I despise that 'NONE OF THE ABOVE'. I cringe every time I see 'NONE OF THE ABOVE'. I went all summer long without one time running across 'NONE OF THE ABOVE' and I had really forgotten that 'NONE OF THE ABOVE' even existed when all of a sudden here it is like a dark cloud hanging over my life. 'NONE OF THE ABOVE'.

Just what exactly does 'NONE OF THE ABOVE' mean anyway? It means there are Nine Hundred Ninety-Nine Million Billion GigaZillion other possible answers, that's what it means. It means the Vegas Odds are that any other answer you choose is wrong. It means that all the other possible choices can be pretty darn close, *extremely* darn close, but just not quite the perfect one. Personally, I think it means the professor couldn't come up with anything else clever.

'NONE OF THE ABOVE' means sixteen is the possible answer. 'NONE OF THE ABOVE' means knish is the possible answer. But ask any professor what 'NONE OF THE ABOVE' means and they will, invariably without a doubt, tell you this: "It means you didn't study enough." Ouch!

But just how is it possible to study enough for 'NONE OF THE ABOVE'? How is it humanly possible to prepare oneself for all the mathematical possibilities 'NONE OF THE ABOVE' encompasses? It is impossible, I say. Impossible! A person would have to read every book in the Newman Library and even then he/she would only be scratching the surface of what 'NONE OF THE ABOVE' is. You never see 'NONE OF THE ABOVE' on Jeopardy. Why? Because "What is 'NONE OF THE ABOVE'?" has never been defined in a controlled laboratory environment. That's why.

And furthermore, what does 'NONE OF THE ABOVE' teach us? Some say nothing. Nada. Zilch. Others argue we learn lots from 'NONE OF THE ABOVE'. At this very moment there is extensive 'NONE OF THE ABOVE' research going on at some major colleges and universities around this country, including Harvard Tech in Flatbush, Arkansas. Professors there have set up a controlled environment laboratory classroom experiment dealing with the question of the answer 'NONE OF THE ABOVE', examining its effects on society and the mating habits of the South American Horned Toed Frog. Following is an excerpt of a transcript taken from one such experimental classroom:

Student#1: Professor Plinghammer, would that be the alpha letter 'S' or the numeric number '5' that you just wrote on the blackboard?

Prof Plinghammer: It is a seven, or an eight, or 'NONE OF THE ABOVE'.

Student#1: Thank-you Dr. Plinghammer. Will this be on the test?

Prof Plinghammer: Yes, no, maybe, or 'NONE OF THE ABOVE'.

Student#1: Thank-you Dr. Plinghammer.

Student#2: Professor Plinghammer is brilliant. He really makes me think.

Student#3: Yes, and his nose hairs really turn me on.

Yes, it is obvious to see why 'NONE OF THE ABOVE' is being so hotly debated by some of the greatest minds in this country. According to the Presidential Council on Public Education, this extensive 15-year study has been commissioned to determine if:

A: 'NONE OF THE ABOVE' ***IS*** beneficial to the educational process.

B: 'NONE OF THE ABOVE' ***IS NOT*** beneficial to the educational process.

C: 'NONE OF THE ABOVE'.

Until this 15-year study is up, I suppose I am stuck with 'NONE OF THE ABOVE'. And if 'NONE OF THE ABOVE' isn't enough, darn if ALL OF THE ABOVE doesn't show up every now and then too. Not to mention the A&B or B&D, or A,C,&D, all members of that notorious gang better known as SOME OF THE ABOVE. So there I sit staring all of them in the face, 'NONE OF THE ABOVE', ALL OF THE ABOVE, SOME OF THE ABOVE, each one just as repulsive as the other, and to keep from screaming bloody murder I close my eyes, take in a deep breath, and summon up THE FORCE LUKE, THE FORCE. Then I flip a coin.

'NONE OF THE ABOVE', the professor's wildcard, should be against the law!

Yes, that 'NONE OF THE ABOVE' is some nasty business ...

...BUSINESS

And while in college is when I first set about the business of changing the world and took my first stab at political commentary. I took that first stab about the same time O.J. Simpson was taking his, and he made out okay so why shouldn't I? My stab was printed in the big city paper, the *Roanoke Times and World News*, on August 3, 1998. It took up a full half page of the commentary section. They added a really neat illustration of a man hunched over from the weight of an elderly college professor in cap and gown riding on his back.

The title in big bold print said *College Presidents' Salaries Soar, But Not Others.* It went like this:

Today at Virginia Tech, the President of the college makes $246,000.00 per year in straight salary. By straight salary, I mean his paycheck only. This figure does not include all his perks such as free lodging and transportation in addition to his stipends for board memberships and speaking engagements. Conversely, a starting custodian, housekeeper, or dining hall worker (or any other Grade 1 position) hired in at Virginia Tech makes $11,932.00 per year. This figure includes all perks.

Right now, the President of Virginia Tech makes 21 times that of a Grade 1 employee. Nearly 20 years ago in 1981, the ratio of the President's salary in relation to the lowest paid worker's was about 7:1. Since 1981, the salary of the President of Virginia Tech has more than tripled (an increase of $172,000.00) while the salary of a Grade 1 worker has *virtually remained the same for two decades* (an increase of only $1,686.00 over 17 years)! Wow! The salary of the upper tier at Virginia Tech seems to be exponentially rising. Nothing like hitting the 21st Century at Warp Speed!!

Is the economy booming that much in America? Is personal wealth rising like never before? I seem to recall having seen reports claiming that the dollar bill has less spending power today than it did 20 years ago. This is good for some, bad for others. Into which category do you fall? If it bothers you that milk costs you three dollars a gallon as opposed to two dollars a gallon, then you need to read on. If the price of a bag of groceries is no concern of yours, then stop here and stick your head back down into the sand.

Though the cost of living has steadily increased over the past 20 years in America, the lowest pay rate at Virginia Tech has virtually stayed put. Were these Grade 1 workers grossly overpaid 20 years ago? I doubt it. One might argue that the number of laborers required at Virginia Tech has increased substantially over the past 20 years, thus requiring the wages paid to remain relatively low to compensate for the increase in numbers of workers. There is some truth to this of course as this is simple economics. However, I am willing to bet that the number of administrators has increased in relative proportion to the number of laborers, if not more so. So why only sharp increases in administrative salaries?

Have there been leaps and bounds in the impact of Virginia Tech on society, thus warranting windfall rewards? Though I am happy to say there have been many positive gains, I don't recall any recent Virginia Tech graduates curing the common cold. Come to think of it, I don't recall any recent Harvard or Yale graduates doing so either. What has taken place over the past 20 years that warrants a 300 percent increase in prosperity for some and 100 percent stagnation for others?

According to a recent Washington Post article from Sunday, May 17, 1998, Virginia's Governor Gilmore wants to cut spending waste at colleges in the state. Gilmore is beginning a wholesale review of finances at Virginia universities that senior aides say could lead to creation of a powerful new state panel to tighten controls on how the schools spend $1.3 billion a year. "He's concerned about the unregulated outflow of cash" from the state to the schools, said one member of Gilmore's inner circle. "It's the constant dollar chase by each university that bothers him. It's not centered on the students; it's on prestige."

According to the same article, nationally, presidents' salaries at four-year schools average about $170,000.00, while those at large research institutions such as U-Va. average $330,000.00. The President of UVA makes $301,000.00 per year plus $45,000.00 deferred pay with lodging and car, Virginia Tech's President is listed at $255,000.00 (my figures differ slightly because they are from a 12/97 payroll list) plus lodging, transportation, and club memberships.

So where does the Governor wish to begin his cuts? Does he wish to further deplete the already scaled down, bare boned maintenance and housekeeping crews which keep things operating smoothly, help feed, clean and pick up after our future doctors and lawyers? Does he wish to further deplete the already depleted number of actual instructors who must teach classes containing hundreds of students at a time? Does he wish to cut back spending on desks and classroom accessories? Cut back any more on maintenance and facilities and you directly deprive the students themselves. Not a very good idea, I'd say.

But why such large pay increases at Virginia Tech? A boom in the economy has brought about utopia perhaps? Great, I'm glad that administration could benefit! I'm all for progress and improvement. Perhaps a massive pay raise is presently being drawn up for the lower grades at Virginia Tech, and I'm just flying off the handle here. If so, then I say it is about time they got their due. Let the laborers benefit from the good times too.

And what about the instructors at Virginia Tech? I don't believe many salaries have tripled over the past 20 years as has administrations. A handful of professor's salaries have jumped quite substantially, but it seems they are in the administrative positions in their respective departments. If anyone should be seeing a 300% rise in their paychecks it surely should be the actual teachers themselves, should it not?!?

Is Virginia Tech administration merely attempting to keep pace with the private business administrative sector? Although Virginia Tech is a business in many, many ways, it is nonetheless a "non profit" institution of higher learning. If Virginia Tech wishes to be a private business and behave like private business, then that's ok by me. Simply stop giving my tax dollars to Virginia Tech and all will be forgotten. However, as long as Virginia Tech is a state supported institution funded by taxpayer dollars from the citizens of this Commonwealth of Virginia, then I suggest that it begin implementing a more *common wealth* payroll scheme by which to take care of more of its hard working employees. Obviously the money is there- it is simply being unfairly distributed *to* those in power *by* those in power.

The Virginia Military Institute recently had talked of going exclusively private in order to resist public scrutiny and remain entirely male. This did not happen because V.M.I. knows it must have the support and backing of the taxpayers of Virginia. Ditto for Virginia Tech. And just as the Virginia Military Institute was forced to conform to the will of the people of this Commonwealth, so too should Virginia Tech.

Now, taking all the above into consideration, is Virginia Tech guilty of any wrongdoing? Not at all. Virginia Tech is no guiltier than any other college in Virginia, or the country for that matter. Virginia Tech is no guiltier of shortchanging its workers than IBM or McDonalds. The fact is, Virginia Tech is simply following right along in the footsteps of big business and corporate America where the CEOs are getting richer and richer by the day at the expense of the working class.

So what is my beef? My beef is that I expect more from Virginia Tech. I expect better from an institution whose very premise is to improve the quality of life for mankind- all mankind. I expect Virginia Tech to stand up for democracy. I expect Virginia Tech to take the lead in doing the right thing.

Instead, I see Virginia Tech falling right in line with all the rest of this country's philosophy of elitism and subjugation, adding fuel to the ever-increasing gap between the "have and have-nots." I see an elite group of individuals getting richer and richer at the expense of others. I see the rich and powerful pulling out all the stops in America and sprinting across the carcasses of the masses as they squash their way to the top. I see this country heading backward into the days of royalty and serfdom. And if you would but open your eyes, you would see it too.

I am a Hokie, and always want to be. But above that, I am a human being. I am a Virginian. I live in Virginia. I am an American. I live in America. I am an Earthling. I live on the planet Earth. I believe in living peacefully side by side with my neighbor. I also believe in treating my neighbor with fairness, dignity, and respect. Does Virginia Tech offer any courses on that? They have nothing...

...NOTHING

I never wanted to have it all in life, but to have nothing at the age of forty-three is a bit demoralizing. "Why try?" I ask myself. It doesn't matter how hard you try. Starting from nothing and working hard leaves you farther behind then starting with lots and hardly working. It's a fact. Work does not earn capital nowadays. Capital earns capital. America has become one big accounting gimmick and work and labor are secondary.

People with money play golf and get richer while workers work and grow worst off.

Affirmative action is a program that was designed to help bridge the gap between the rich and the poor, but it has come under attack as of late by whites being left behind in the race for the world's wealth. These whites, an ever growing percentage of the population, are too ignorant to see that it is not the fault of the poor black who is getting a chance, it is the fault of the prosperous white who is making the rules and taking more and more for himself while leaving the crumbs for you poor white trash and the black to battle over.

And while the race battle rages on in America, colleges clandestinely use institutionalized affirmative action to admit children of affluent families in order to gain favor in the family estates. There has been a substantial increase in fundraising efforts across today's college campuses in America. The philosophy is that if you ask one hundred people for money you will at least get one to contribute something. Therefore, if you ask the entire world, you could strike it rich.

The college began asking anyone and everyone for money. Twice. Sometimes thrice a year. Graduates of the college were called on the phone, sent mailings, newsletters, all focused on trying to drum up some sort of donation. The alumni fund spun off into the parents fund where parents of students attending school were asked to give money, money above and beyond the money they were already doling out to keep their child in school. Then there came the senior fund where graduating seniors were asked to give money despite the fact that they were still in school and not earning any money yet. The whole premise behind the senior fund was more a conditioning, or programming, or indoctrination of the college student into the world of charitable philanthropy. And its tax write-offs, of course.

Because after all, write-off is the name of the game.

I worked in a fund raising division of a college once, and in the seven years I was there I watched the place grow dramatically around me. Hundreds upon hundreds of students were brought in to call people at night and beg for money for the college. There was a program known as the Alumni Campaign. This is a pretty standard fund raising campaign that can be found at practically every college in the country. People who graduated from the college, otherwise known as the college's alumni, are called and asked to give, or pay back as it were, to the college in order for it to continue to educate tomorrow's leaders.

This in itself is a gallant endeavor and I see no harm in a graduate of the college giving something back to the institution that propelled him or her into society's fray. However, from what I saw taking place they could have changed the name of Alumni Hall all about baby. As the fund raising frenzy grew within the college, it became a dumping ground for major corporations to dispose of old equipment and outdated or unmarketable technology in return for tax breaks from the government. A major company like IBM or McDonnell Douglas could give the college some software that had been developed, but no longer used, by the company, appraise it at some astronomical figure despite the fact that the technology is useless to them, and receive a large break on their taxes because of their donation to the university. Software, used equipment, land, all these things fall into an ambiguous value category and are thus easily overvalued in order for the big corporation to come out ahead.

And is the college going to say no to any sort of donation? Of course they won't. They will take it any way they can get it.

I recall once a situation where an alumni, a wealthy alumni, was in the twilight of his life and was working on including the college in his will. There was quite a bit of correspondence going back and forth between the attorneys of the college and the elderly alumni's attorneys. The gist of the correspondence was that the man, who had had a falling out with his children some years before, was thinking of leaving all of his money to the university while essentially cutting his children out of everything.

I personally found this to be the pathetic ranting of senile old man. I could not see how anyone would want to, could want to cut their own children out of their estate. However, the lawyers in our offices were working at a feverish pace in order to nail down a signed, sealed agreement before the man reconciled with his children.

Now what kind of shit is that I ask you? Is there no honor at all amongst thieves? It seemed to me that our college should have been encouraging the man to reconcile with his children while also including the college in his will. But instead, we would cut his children out in order to gain more.

How low is that I ask you? I guess to some reading this, it is business. But to me, I think it stinks and I can only hope that anyone who is low enough to do something like this will have it done to them one day.

While I worked in the office there was this one department there that handled all the parties. Planning these parties was a pretty big deal, and they would sit for hours and days and weeks planning out the seating arrangements at the tables. There are so many issues that go into seating arrangements then meet the untrained eye. There are issues like:

1.) Is subject A pretty enough to sit with subject B?
2.) Is subject A affluent enough to sit with subject B?
3.) Is subject A comfortable with the color of subject B's skin?

Of course there are other important factors to consider, factors like who is left-handed and who is right handed, and who is large and who is small. You don't want to seat all the large people in one place or they will take offense at being seated with someone who looks as bad as they do. All these issues take a trained decision maker experienced in the art of dining for dollars.

This department would spend hours having lunch and while an untrained eye might have thought that they were mere merely having a long lunch they were in fact studying and debating and absorbing all the little intricacies involved with eating and talking while talking and eating.

It was a tough assignment, and only a select few were called for duty. These were an elite bunch they were, and weeks upon weeks of planning for parties paled in comparison to the grueling assignment of the party itself where all this preparation comes to a head and the rubber meets the road as the bottoms meet their seat and the night becomes one orgasmic calliope of wine and cheese and wine and song and more wine and crackers and wine and some dancing and falling down carefully as not to spill the wine.

These special recruits were usually of upper crust breeding. The girls were always pretty, and the guys were always your classic fraternity franks. There was this one fellow who interned in the party department. He was a nice guy with a square jaw, attractive smile, and warm personality to go along with it all. I couldn't stand him.

I was seething with jealousy but what could I do? He was a real favorite at parties and I was a real knot on a log, so what the hell could I say. The kid was an up and comer, and he could play the hell out of some golf too. So why did I hate him so? He never did anything bad to me that I could speak of. I imagine he had some clever comments behind my back, but I can't swear to that, so my comments about him behind his back are given with the understanding that they only count if he said something first.

And I still liked the guy and his fellow workers when I found out that they were being paid for taking lunch because this was part of their job, and they were getting paid while attending the parties and functions involved with all the fundraisers.

I never got paid to go somewhere for lunch. I never even had just my lunch paid for. I was only a man working trying to support two children and attend school, their school, in order to better myself, but all their concessions and perks and favors went to the young party planners who were more accustomed and acclimated to getting it all as fast as they could take it in. But anyway, it is not that I hated the kid. It was not his fault for being born privileged. We always spoke hello to each other at first (until he was given 'the package deal') and even exchanged some email regarding dirty jokes and an assortment of smut. We talked from time to time around the coffee pot as all office personnel are prone to do from time to time, and we were discussing the game of tennis and I learned that he had grown up with a tennis court in his back yard. I had never met anyone that I knew of who had his own tennis court. I didn't have anything against it, but I guess it bothered me a bit when he said he never used it because he was always too busy playing golf.

But I still liked the guy and we continued to be friends in the office until I started seeing the way that he and the others in the party department were allowed to do their homework and play on the internet all day long (when they weren't at lunch or planning parties) and I was not allowed do anything of the sort. I can't tell you the number of times I walked by their department on my way to retrieve a file and someone would be doing homework or surfing the internet or playing solitaire on the computer. I played solitaire once while I was on break, and the next day a memo came out prohibiting the playing of solitaire during working hours, and the games were removed from my computer. The party department received no such memo and they carried on as usual.

But who was I to complain but a lowly pedophile lucky to have a job at all? So just keep your mouth shut and mind your business. I wish I could have...

...COULD HAVE

I wish I could have just accepted things the way they were and minded my own business. I recall the first instance when I was faced with just accepting things the way they were and minding my own business, and as a young boy it left an impression on me. There was this dark-skinned boy about my age who would come visit with our next-door neighbors sometimes. There was an Army General's or Colonel's or something's family who lived there, a white family, and my parents said the black boy was related to that white family somehow. The General or Colonel or whatever was always in his uniform whenever I saw him, which wasn't very often, and he always had this mean look on his face and was always yelling about something so I stayed out of his way.

The Army guy's own son and I were pals and we played outdoors or over at my house a lot, but I didn't like going over to his house very much because his dad was always yelling at him and was very strict with him. We would always have to play very quiet and keep things very neat in his room whenever we played inside his house, and it just goes against kid's nature, so consequently we got, or he got, yelled at a lot any time we played inside their house so we didn't do it much. My parents were much more laid back and easy-going, albeit in charge, and other kids from around the neighborhood would play over at my place. Of course, it didn't hurt that I had one of the flattest back yards in the neighborhood. It must have been only a hundred or so feet wide, but for a few summers there before we grew bigger and faster it seemed like a real football field to us kids.

Getting back to my story, this dark skinned kid would visit and he was the first dark-skinned person I had ever known and he was really cool, and lots of fun to play with. He was energetic and competitive and always had this big smile on his face as if to say everything was okay. But everything wasn't okay because the Army General or whatever he was used to spank the crap out of that poor little dark skinned boy, and though he was also strict on his own son, he was out of control when it came to that black kid who was related to him in some fashion. He would order the boy back over to their house and then scream at him and beat on him until I wanted to cry. And my mom would make us (me and my brother and sister) come inside when the General started yelling at his nephew or grandson or whoever he was. And I would ask my mom why the Army guy was so mean to that little dark-skinned boy and my mom could never give me an answer except to look sad and say that she felt sorry for the boy but it was none of our business.

I never really was sure if I ever got a definite answer as to who that dark-skinned kid was exactly, as if it was a big mystery and no one was supposed to know who he really was and how he was related to the General's or whatever family.

My memories of that dark-skinned boy are vague, and that Army guy's family didn't stay there long before they moved away and I never saw my friend or his dad or the little dark-skinned boy again.

This was the first brush with having to bite my tongue and accept something despite knowing it was wrong...

...WRONG

There are some things in America that are just flat out wrong. America can be a very confusing place to grow up in. America claims to be the land of the free, yet curfews and fences and restrictions are everywhere. America claims to be the most powerful nation on Earth, yet it is in debt up to its ears to the Japanese. America claims to be the leader in civil rights, yet its recent history with the Indians and blacks refutes that, not to mention its sticking its nose into other countries business all over the globe. Yes, if nothing else, America has become the land of the fee and home of the hypocrite. It is just not right.

Many people today attribute the recent rash of school killings as a breakdown of morals in America. Jerry Falwell, the Baptist Minister from Virginia and self-proclaimed leader of the country's so-called moral majority, would have you believe that the homosexuals are behind it all. God forbid people of the same sex could fall in love with each other. Although I don't prescribe to that lifestyle, I do believe it is possible for people of the same sex to be in love. I don't understand it, and there was a time in my life when I thought homosexuality was wrong. My argument against it was that if all men loved men and women loved women, then the human race would come to an end because there would be no reproduction to carry on the species because it takes a male to fertilize a female egg. When very young, us guys would play a game called 'Smear the Queer.' The game was pretty simple- whoever held the football would get body slammed by everyone else until he gave up the ball and it was someone else's turn to get hammered. I guess it was just instilled into me at an early age that being gay was not cool.

But as I grew older I realized that gay was just another way of life, and I found myself becoming sympathetic towards gay people. I found out that there were gays all over the place. People who I would never have guessed to be gay were gay. The stereotypes of men in their tight yellow pants and flowered silk shirts were shattered when guys like Rock Hudson and J. Edgar Hoover were exposed as being gay. Some people I worked with along the way were gay. They were always some of the nicest people.

I also came to learn that I had things in common with gays. Being that I am attracted to black women instead of blondes, I found myself an outcast in some circles. I recall a conversation with an older woman I worked with. It was back in the mid-eighties, and the gay revolution (if you want to call it that) was just getting started. "I'm gay and I'm proud" was the theme, and more and more people were coming out of their closets and telling the world about their secret. We were discussing the trend, and I said that I didn't like to see two men walking down the street holding hands. The woman, who I admired and enjoyed working with, told me that she could stomach it much easier than seeing a black and white couple walking down the street. She didn't say it with malice and she knew that I was married to a black woman, just as I did not make my statement about gay men with malice. We were both just being honest and stating how we felt.

But it made me realize (even more than I already did) how much Americans are brainwashed into prejudice without even knowing it. It sort of surprised me to learn that some people thought less of a heterosexual relationship between races than they did a homosexual relationship wherever. And I saw that where I had grown up playing 'smear the queer', she may have grown up playing 'hang that nigger,' and it made me sad to think what a pathetic bunch of idiots are we all.

People talk about the decline of morals yet where were morals in America when blacks were being hanged by the thousands each year in the South? Where were the morals when the Indians had their lands and the buffalo taken from them by a civilized breed called Caucasian? Where were morals when blacks were denied the right to vote as recently as the 1960's? Where were the morals when young men were sent to die for nothing in Vietnam? If morals are on the decline in America, then we are now below the bottom.

It is not morals; it is confusion that is causing all the chaos. We grow up watching game shows on television give away hundreds of thousands of dollars daily, yet we are asked to go out on Halloween and collect pennies for starving families because every penny counts. We grow up watching blockbuster movies that cost millions upon millions of dollars to produce, yet families live in poverty because businesses can't afford to pay them a decent wage. Is it little wonder that children are 'going ballistic' in record numbers today? Children see politicians break the law and get away with it. Children see their friends from well to do families break the law and get away with it. Children see that killing is wrong, yet they see America bombing innocent people on foreign lands.

Children in America today are confused. And the recent rash of well-to-do white males snapping and shooting their schools up makes one wonder if our children are ever really safe anywhere...

...SAFE ANYWHERE

Are our children safe anywhere? The question is being asked from coast to coast in America. Following school shootings in Jonesboro Arkansas, West Paducah Kentucky, Pearl Mississippi, Springfield Oregon, and more recently Columbine High School in Littleton Colorado, parents everywhere are desperate to know why children are snapping in growing numbers. Parents are frantic to insure their neighborhood schoolyards are safe, all the while asking are our children safe at school? But I ask you America, are our children safe at home?

Are our children safe at home with parents who are so caught up in their careers and their struggle for power and prestige that they don't even know their children exist? Are our children safe from professionals who are able to provide sumptuous shelter, bountiful buffet, and opulent opportunity for their children, yet who alienate them and become blind to the arsenals being amassed and the hatred being cultivated right under their very noses? What if these children simply disappeared? How many days or weeks would pass before their self-absorbed parents noticed they are missing? Are our children safe at home?

Are our children safe from parents who adamantly condemn violence, who penalize physical altercation of any kind (including defending ones self) on school property with out-of-school suspension, then who turn around and profit from the manufacture and distribution of land mines and weaponry? Are our children safe at home from parents who preach that life is so very precious, then turn around and drop bombs on some poor county's innocent citizens because a ruling madman is running loose amongst them? Are our children safe at home?

Kids today are not stupid, especially these kids who snapped. They were all intelligent children from well-to-do families. All were given anything they asked for by their parents. What caused these young children to hate the world enough to kill, and themselves enough to die? Had their spoiled existence become so effortless and mundane that it lost any meaning? Did their parent's apparent lack of interest cause these children to feel unloved and invisible? Were these atrocities committed as a way to get attention? If so then what a sad pathetic senseless reason for their victims to die.

Are our children safe from parents who talk of morality and respect, who donate to all the right causes, who buy Barney's *Sharing is Caring* video to play over and over, then who turn around and orchestrate a lay-off of hundreds of their companies workers in order to reap a large stock dividend for themselves to pay for another lavish vacation to exotica, or a new summer home? And are they safe from parents who spout off about fairness and equality while all the while basking in the warm glow of elitist luxuriance and country club camaraderie. Are our children safe from a capitalistic society that encourages these elitist beliefs?

Are our children safe from parents who want so badly to provide a safe, stable environment for their own that they move their families farther away from the violent war-zones that are our inner-city neighborhoods, thereby exacerbating the problems they leave behind. It costs money to live in the posh neighborhoods that make up the mid to upper class in America, and the more money taken in by the upper-crust spells less for the depressed neighborhoods that these elitists are so desperate to get away from. Isn't it ironic that the very violence that is an everyday reality for oppressed, the very violence that America's well-to-do have turned their back on, has somehow found its way into their own sheltered environments? Are our children safe at home?

And what of possible drug use by these children? Are our children safe at home with parents who implore "just say no just say no to drugs" while at the same time popping everything from anti-depressant pills to hair growing enhancement into their mouth? America has become inundated by 'legal', fast-track drugs being shoved in our face everyday. Health segments, endorsed by the American Medical Association and the National Association for the Advancement of Doctoral Greed, peddle a virtual plethora of overrated, always revolutionary, always under-tested, ever expensive miracle drugs to the American public young and old. These drugs promise to cure everything from cancer or depression, to stupidity. Children see America's love affair with prescription drugs and wonder why their locker is being searched for a joint. One former presidential candidate is even a spokesman for Viagra, the new miracle cure for erectile dysfunction, or E.D. Shame on you, Bob. You don't even mention that it could blow up your heart. Buy a Playboy, or just say no, Bob. Are our children safe at home?

Yet, despite all its hypocrisy, children need to see that America is still the best of all possible worlds. America is the greatest nation on earth with its ample resources, democratic society, and amber waves of grain. But America has issues that need to be addressed, and it is high time the privileged elite who control it address them.

It is time to address the flaws in our society that are increasing the gap between the have and have-nots and polarizing Americans more and more while at the same time breeding prejudice, hatred and discontent. Columbine High School is proof that no group is exempt.

Yes, it is time for Americans to come together and address issues larger than the President's penis. It is time to make our homes safe for our children. It is time.

It is time to end the confusion. White children see young blacks who they like (the forces of nature) but they feel they cannot be their friend because their parents or friends might not approve of it.

Young white boys see their black schoolmates who are so very fast, or so very athletic, or so very handsome, and they do not understand why they are not as fast or strong or good looking or popular with the girls. After all, aren't they supposed to be superior to the black?

Children hear love your neighbor as yourself, then they are spoon-fed Jerry Falwell with his bigotry and prejudice and they are confused.

Children are told that with hard work they will get ahead, then they see that sitting on one's ass and gambling with money on the stock market is really the way to get ahead, and work is for some other poor sucker, and they are confused.

It is all about confusion. It's confusing as hell I tell you...

...TELL YOU

I want to tell you about that night – that night that caused me to be accused then convicted of aggravating and sexually assaulting a young innocent underage girl. The night would have been a Friday or Saturday night because my oldest son had a couple of his teammates from his sandlot football team over to spend the night and it wouldn't have been a night where they had to go to school the following morning. One of the boys happened to be April's younger brother and when he showed up that evening April was with him, along with her cousin.

They all came in and the kids gravitated into the back bedroom to play while April and her cousin and I stayed up front in the living room to talk. I was totally thrilled to see her again, and she looked every bit as lovely as the first time I had seen her. We sat and watched TV and she talked about school with her cousin and I just watched and listened mostly. I thought she had just walked over with her brother to drop him off and would not be staying long but then she told me that she wasn't doing anything that night and that she was hoping they could hang out for a while.

Now my heart began to race a bit. Where only a few minutes earlier I had been hoping there was a good movie on TV so that I could get lost in it now here was this beautiful young lady that I was interested in sitting in front of me looking quite fetching and now my mind began to wander. I was still a married man and still in love with my wife, but she was unfaithful and had made it clear she didn't want me anymore and so perhaps it was time to face the facts and get on with my life.

I watched April with interest and our eyes met and held each other's gaze for long periods of time and I was torn inside with what to do. I could tell from her eyes that she was there to spend some time with me and I was not sure if it would be right or not but I was dying to hold her and be comforted by her. I wanted her badly yet I knew that if I gave in to her I would be giving up on my marriage and my wife entirely and I was not sure if I wanted that or not. I knew my wife didn't love me anymore, yet I didn't want to accept it. I didn't want to give up on my marriage.

I had made a vow to myself that I would not let my marriage end in divorce. I was the child of divorced parents and I had promised myself that I would never put my own kids through that misery. But here now was decision time. How long could I continue to take the abuse I was taking from my Carolyn? I needed to break away, and here was my chance. It's time to move on.

My mind raced and my nerves frazzled and I sat there staring at April wondering if she could be the one and I needed some time to think so I asked the girls if they could stay there with the kids while I went out for a little while. I needed to get away to think clearly, so I did what any man does when he needs to think clearly, I headed for a bar to have a drink. Being that April was a high school senior I didn't think twice about her being able to watch the boys while I went out for a bit.

I stayed out long enough to have a few drinks and mull over what to do. I did still love my wife, but I had been dealing with her infidelity and abuse for over two years now and it was only getting worst. It was obvious to everyone else that she no longer loved me so why wouldn't I admit it and move on? This was my chance. I was very attracted to April and wondered if I could love her like I had loved my wife. I felt almost as attracted to her as I had to my wife, almost the same energy, so I believed that there just might be a chance. Just maybe.

And as if the married thing was not enough to have to work out in my head, there was another slight matter that was disconcerting, or uncomfortable, for me. Her age. April was young. She was only seventeen and a high school senior and despite the fact that her eighteenth birthday was only two weeks away she was still a minor. The legalities of this didn't really bother me that much because girls were married all the time at sixteen in the old days, and if she really cared for me then her being seventeen would not matter. And in a matter of days she would be eighteen and legally a woman.

However, it did bother me that she was so young and I was much older and with children. I wondered if she really knew what she was getting into. I wondered if she would be ready to accept the responsibility of a 'ready-made family.' I wondered if she would only be around long enough to make me fall for her and then run away like my wife had done.

I had a few drinks to calm my nerves and wondered what to do, wondered what is the right thing to do, then I paid my bill and headed back home. I wondered would April be waiting up for me. I hoped she would be waiting up for me...

...FOR ME

Things have gone from bad to worst for me now as I am still unable to secure gainful employment. My days are filled with almost absolute boredom now. I sit at my computer and browse the net or play games; I watch TV or play some on my keyboard. I feel as though I get nothing accomplished, nothing constructive that is. I suppose, though, that every minute is constructive in itself.

I'll watch each movie that I see not only as a viewer but also as a director or cameraman as well. I'll pay close attention to detail and remember scenes that stand out from the rest just in case I want to get the same affect in one of my own films. I look at commercials and analyze what it is that makes them a winner or loser in my book, making sure to jot down a mental note to myself just in case I want to use the same tricks in my own commercials.

I browse the net and keep tabs on the heartbeat of America. I peruse the forums to see how deep and how wide is the shit today. I look to see what is the latest venom being spewed forth by all the fanatical idiots who have found a soapbox and a place to blow off steam in the Internet. And once I've finished blowing off my own steam I make a mental note to check back at the website later to see if I have been able to stir up any hornet's nests which is the underlying goal to begin with. I look to see what the latest is from the New York Times Online, and always I read between the lines of America's number one propaganda pipeline.

I walk the dog, another mundane task that has become my life. We go on the same square circuit every time, and every time the dog attempts to pull away from the leash and run off to freedom. Actually, I do allow him to run sometimes. I take him on a walk around this pond and there is a large, wide open, grassy field beside it where I will let him run free. Once I unhook the leash from his collar, he always stops after a few excited steps to test the leash, then a few more tentative steps quicker this time until once he is sure the leash will not hold him back he takes off like a cannon shot. With his nose cutting the wind and his ears pinned back against his head, he flies around the field with the look of pure ecstasy on his face and in his eyes. I would like to know how it feels to be able to run with the wind. What a great feeling it must be. And to do it naked!

Dogs don't realize how lucky they have it. They've got someone waiting on them hand and foot twenty-four hours a day and they never have to pay for a damn bit of it. Their favorite pastimes are eating, sleeping and having sex whenever they damn well please. They never have to answer to any incriminating accusations or to any accusations at all for that matter. When they meet one of heir own kind on the street they never have to worry about making a good impression or not - one quick sniff of the ass tells them everything they need to know. Wow! Dogs almost have it as good as politicians!

After walking the dog I will get back to the computer or back to a movie, or sometimes I will sit down at my electronic keyboards and belt out a masterpiece that would surely be a hit if only I had an audience. I'll play for a while until I get bored with it then go back to the computer or the television. And back to being bored.

It is a humiliating feeling to be here when my son arrives home every day from school. I wonder is he curious why his father is not at a job like all the rest of the fathers are. I do not enjoy sitting here day in and day out feeling so worthless. I know I could go out and get some sort of job washing dishes or cleaning floors or something like that but I just went to college for five years to get a degree and I would really like to think that it allows me to do something that pays better. I had done my share of menial labor in my life I wanted more.

I wouldn't mind doing menial labor but it is so underpaid unfortunately in America. I think that it should pay more than administration but administration has the power and the control of the payroll and so they always give themselves more.

I am becoming more irritable and my patience is wearing thin...

...THIN

I still cannot get through to the Department of Social Services Support Enforcement Division for two days now and my patience is wearing thin. The Department of Social Services is a prime example of a state run organization that is in pathetic shape. But of course, they do this on purpose because they want their customers to become fed up with them and go the alternate route, the alternate route being make it on your own.

Where is the damn child support I am supposed to be getting? I know its not much but right now every little bit helps.

Trying to get through to speak to an actual human being at this agency is like trying to find a four-leaf clover- you just have to be lucky. You have to be lucky not to get a busy signal. If you are lucky and get a ring, you are welcomed by an automated answering system's synthetic voice that gives you options to choose from. If you want to speak to a case worker, you are transferred to a busy signal if you are not lucky. If you are lucky, you will not get the busy signal but silence instead. Dead silence. This silence will go on for days if you let it, but the best plan is to hang up and start again. It is unbelievable.

Once, I got past the first busy signal and then the second busy signal and instead of the silence I got a ringing phone. The phone rang and rang. I let it ring for about five minutes and no one ever picked up. I finally hung up and tried again.

Again no luck.

Fuck. Why should I have to suffer like this when I am the one taking care of these kids? Why should I always have to do all the struggling when Support Services should be bending over backwards for me, me a single father raising his children, not the typical 'deadbeat dad' they spend the majority of their time chasing after. Why should I be made to suffer? Shouldn't the absent mother be the one made to suffer a bit for bailing out on her children?

I tried the number again but no luck.

Where is my got damned child support check!?!

Does she think this is all just a game...

...GAME

I don't want to play this game anymore. I have grown so weary of being a single parent. I no longer have any motivation to keep on. I don't want a job I don't even want to get up in the morning. But even worst, I don't want to just lie in bed that is contrary to my nature. I can't sit still for long, unless I can get wrapped up in a good movie. But even that doesn't pacify me like it used to. There is an unsettled feeling in my bones and I know what it is.

I don't want to play this game anymore. I am tired of being a single parent. It is not that I don't love my children anymore it is just that I am tired of having all of the responsibility placed squarely on my shoulders. My shoulders are not that broad. I am tired of having to be the one to make all the decisions. I am tired of being the one who has to do all the scolding. I am tired of being the one who has to handle all the paperwork, registration and fees, rent in on time, wash the clothes, make sure they get fed, cared for during sickness... I grow weary of it all because I am so miserably lonely. I am so tired of being miserable and alone.

I want to have fun again in life. I want to be able to take a weekend for myself and go play golf like lots of people I know do. I want to travel to the away games and party it up all game and all night like so many people I know do. I want to treat myself to a shopping spree and spend hundreds of dollars to lift my spirits and let me know that, yes Virginia, there is a God. But why don't I you ask. Why don't I just do all these things that I want to do? Because I just don't have that spending cash on me to party like I'd like to. I made some bad decisions along the way, and now I have this child I am carrying on my back and I would like to do things for myself but I can't because my number one priority is to my child and whatever is left over is what I have for myself.

But fun doesn't always have to cost money. I want to go out and pick up a girl and bring her home and run naked all over the apartment. I want to go out and get picked up by a girl and taken to her apartment where we can run naked and lie next to each other when the night meets the morning sun. I want to talk for a while and walk for a while by the sea. But I can't just run off and get involved with anyone because what you see is not what you get - I have children at home and they depend on me and they are waiting for me to come home to cook for them. And I have children at home waiting for me to come back so that they can rest easy and sleep peacefully at night. I have children at home who matter more to me and I must tell you straight up that what you see is not all of it - there is more. So never mind.

I thought I had it all figured out once upon a time. I never wanted to make lots of money to be able to jet around the globe on a whim, I only wanted to get along and pay my way through life. And be happy. Growing up I always thought that a job pumping gas would be a nice profession, but I quickly found out that it didn't pay the bills. I thought that a job in a hardware store or a job as a cashier at the grocery store would be a nice profession, but I learned that they don't pay the bills. I just wanted a job where I could do something constructive and feel useful all day through, but I learned that that type of job does not pay the bills if you want to raise a family. And be happy. No, companies don't pay workers. Companies today pay "schmoozers."

A scholar up north has decided to re-write the Bible by hand. What a momentous occasion for those with nothing better to do. How much money will be devoted towards this frivolous endeavor? How much of my taxes will be diverted away from starving black children, starving white children in order to fund an entire department full of bored white intellectuals with nothing better to do than copy history verbatim? I'm all for the project, however I believe a minimum wage would be more appropriate for a task such as this. And with the money saved, another department could be formed to trace all the pictures. Putting people to work -- that's what it's all about.

Oh please...

...PLEASE

Jarian please go talk to your grandparents today. Talk to your grandmother about your problems. Talk to your grandfather about your financial issues. Maybe they will talk to your mom.

But please just go see them and sit with them a while and talk about yourself. You need this. You don't realize how easy it will be if you just make yourself go.

Please. You must address your anger, your frustration, your agony...

...AGONY

It is agony being a parent and seeing your children suffering over something but not be able to do anything for them. I see my children going through the inevitable ups and downs of dating and relationships and I can't help but wonder if the rejection cast upon them by their mother is not having adverse effects on them in their relationships with members of the opposite sex. My oldest boy has been with the same girl for nearly four years now but it seems that their relationship has changed and I see him hurting and it hurts me too.

Not only do I see my oldest going through his trying times but I see my youngest beginning to tune out as well. He is not the same easy-going, care-what-may man that I used to know. I attribute some of this to the fact that he may view me, his dad, as somewhat of a loser. Most of his friends have parents who are professors or doctors or business owners living in a posh neighborhood with nice cars and money to burn. I am a snowball peddler and convicted pedophile. Despite the fact that he may have once been the "luckiest kid in town" because his dad is Eskimo Joe, as he gets older he surely must see that his dad is a failure.

Throw in the fact that his own mother has shunned him and I can see where this can play havoc on a man's mind as he tries to find his purpose and place in the world. I am trying to do better to provide for him, but because of the hole I have dug for myself, I must face the fact that I may not be able to. Thus, whom do I reach out to?

My oldest boy has now (or so he claims) gotten himself into counseling. Though I feel counseling is a bunch of crap, I do want him to talk to someone and try to release some of his pent-up anger. I know that he needs help, and I have sat down with him and tried to talk with him and reason with him and comfort him and let him know that he is loved, but there is no nurturing in the world quite like the nurturing a loving mother can give, and this is what he could really use now.

If only he could call her. It's been eight years now since you saw her. Yes, why don't you do that Jarian call your mother. I'm sure she could help you. I've got her number here. Call her. It's 5552549...

...5552549

I found myself repeating it over and over. I had zoned out for a moment, repeating that number over and over 5552549, 5552549.

Jarian called her -- he finally called his mom after eight long years of zero communication and she only lashed out at him and wanted to know where he had gotten her phone number. It just killed me. How could she still be so belligerent and hateful to him after so many years of not seeing him at all? It was not easy for Jarian to call her but he did. He made the effort to finally contact her. The boy called his mom after eight years of never seeing or hearing from her because he was going through some tough times with a girlfriend and was hoping for a little tenderness during a tough moment in his life but instead all he received was profanity and threats.

I had heard that she was off the crack cocaine but I guess not I guess she is still in a real mess and there is no need for me to even try to call her myself. I know she could do something for the boys -- her boys. Growing up can be tough enough without what these boys have had to endure. I feel so powerless to help them.

I guess by even addressing this issue I only rub salt in wounds that are deep, and perhaps I shouldn't even consider what I am considering-- that being contacting the boy's mother to see if she could/would talk to them. How sick and pathetic it all sounds having to call a mother to ask her to please be a mother -- absolutely pathetic.

But, for whatever reason I have gotten myself into this pathetic situation where I can't even properly care for two young men and although they have it much better than millions in the world they could have it so much better but for a simple hello from their own mom.

And it eats at me because she left me and it still hurts as you can tell, but I am grown and adults divorce all the time, but for these kids it is not natural and I fear sometimes that it might destroy a part of them inside that can never be replaced or will never be allowed to flourish.

Like I said before, the Carolyn I knew was gone now, the mother they knew is gone now, crack cocaine has taken her over and we need to count our blessings and just move on but it's just the hardest thing to do...

...HARDEST THING

Yes indeed I tell you one of the hardest things about parenting is when to take action and when not to take action. There is an incredibly fine line dividing the two, both being actions of a sort, but even though doing nothing requires no action at all, the ramifications of this non-action action can be every bit of the impact as giving the order for full speed ahead. Knowing when to act or remain still can be the hardest thing imaginable sometimes in parenting. It is not a straightforward, go-through-the-motions type task of everyday life. It is not a chore like getting up from that chair to wash those dirty dishes and clean that kitchen up. It is and entirely different task itself, and it can beat you down.

Knowing when to take action and when to simply sit back and hope, pray for the best can be one of the most agonizing decisions any parent can face. When a parent can see that his/her offspring is screwing up royally, the natural reaction is to jump in and try to help. However, sometimes parent intervention can be the worst thing for children. Parent intervention can be helpful, but do the children learn any lessons when parents jump in to fix everything? From my own observations I have concluded that the more a parent fixes things for their child, the more things that child is prone to break.

A big problem in America today is that children are not held accountable for their actions, especially children of the privileged. These kids who come from mid-to-upper class families have no scruples when it comes to destroying someone else's property.

They know from experience that their parents will pull out their checkbook to cover any damages caused by their irresponsible, immature behavior.

Of course, this all goes back to the fact that many of their parents make money too easily and consequently can afford to buy anything their hearts desire. Money earned (and I use the term earned loosely) from investment of disposable income in the stock market is a prime example of "easy money" being made in America today. When money comes so easily as it does in the bull markets of today the value of consumer goods becomes passe. Things such as clothes, cars, jewelry, and other consumer goods are expected by the children of these under-worked and overpaid parents, rather then hoped for.

However, I did not raise my children to expect to receive whatever they wanted. I did not grow up rich, nor have I become rich. I did not shower my children with gifts in hopes that they would like me. I did a pretty good job at giving my children the basics, and they went through school with pretty much anything the other children had. I did not buy my oldest a car for his high school graduation gift as many of his friend's parents did for theirs, and I feel that this was something my son could not understand. We belonged to the class of American's who are overworked and underpaid by those under-worked and overpaid. I had a constant battle on my hands trying to impress upon my children, my oldest especially, that money did not grow on trees in our household- despite the fact that it seemed to at his friend's.

So the boy had begun going through money like it was water over the past year, and it had become quite alarming to me. I had questioned him on several occasions as to what he was doing with all his money, and all he could ever say was he liked to drink and party too much and that he just couldn't refrain from spending it; a pathetic albeit honest answer.

Then he told me that he had quit working for me. He was upset that I had accused him of taking more than his fair share from the business income, but the fact is that he had. I had left him in charge of the snowball business while I was away on vacation for a month. He was supposed to take the daily receipts for each day and lock them in a safe, minus his share for the day. But he had placed very little money in the safe and partied away the rest. I was expecting to have some money waiting for me when I returned from vacation considering it was one of the hottest summers on record, but instead I had to pull money out of my pocket to give the pool their share, and I was left with nothing. He had made quite a good bit of money while I was away, but he did not pay one dime towards his bills. I wanted to ring his neck.

So anyway, he quit from what I think was a guilty conscience. After I took over again at the pool he stopped by my shop briefly to ask for some money but I adamantly refused to help him I was in danger of getting behind in my bills thanks to his mismanagement of the money while I was away. He wouldn't take no for an answer, so I told him that he was walking around with a chip on his shoulder acting like the world owed him something, and that I didn't appreciate that he had decided that I was the one who must pay up.

So I told him, now twenty years old and fucking up royally, that it was time the other half of his family started doing something for him. I felt that the source of some of his problem was the fact that the situation between him and his mother had never been resolved. She had simply walked out, and I feel he had never totally come to terms with that. Who could? Finally he gave up asking me for money and left. I hoped he was going to go see his grandparents. Life can be so unfair at times...

...UNFAIR

I had certainly seen my own share of unfair. I remember the time me and Carolyn had had another fight over her wanting to go out to meet her friends and me not wanting her to go and so she called her brother Butch to come help her leave and he showed up with a rifle to cover me while Carolyn packed her things to leave. Her brother Butch was no slouch. He sometimes rode horses in rodeos and roped steers. Butchie was stout. I was pretty mad and Butch and I got into a shouting match and he hit me over the head with his rifle butt. There was a sudden explosion on my forehead and I reached up and felt it and when I looked at my hand it had blood on it and still stunned my sudden reflex was to punch him as hard as I could. I remember stepping back after my punch and watching him in front of me with his head down hands covering his face and he slowly looked up at me with fire in eyes, one of his eyes badly swollen and bulging, and he lunged at me and we fell backwards into the living room and into my aquarium that shattered to the floor as we fell to the floor and rolled around wrestling and he beat and beat and beat on me until I couldn't fight anymore and then he picked up a vacuum cleaner and stood over me and was going to smash it down on me but Carolyn told him to stop don't kill me and he stopped and then they both left.

I was a mess laying on the floor and Jarian came out of his bedroom and started crying and helping me up. We both were cleaning my blood and water and glass and fish off of the kitchen floor when a sheriff arrived at my door to arrest me for assault on my brother-in-law.

The warrant had been issued by a magistrate whom also did not like the fact that I was married to a black woman and so he was more than willing to issue the warrant. This magistrate had been the local dog catcher for years in the county and finally was promoted to magistrate and now he had power over things he didn't like and he didn't like me the nigger lover. So I was arrested for getting in a fight in my own home with someone who had brought a gun into my home and who had hit me first.

It just was so unfair.

These charges against me were eventually dropped because Butch did not show up for the hearing and years later we patched things up between us and I consider Butch my friend till this day. Things were just so messed up and confusing back then.

Meanwhile around that same time down the road in a small town a police lieutenant was charged with aggravated sexual battery for climbing into the bed of a sleeping female officer and groping her during an off-duty party with several officers present. She groggily awoke to find him lying on top of her kissing and bear hugging her. Before she could even react he had shoved his hand down inside her pants and underneath her panties and began groping her. The female officer jumped up and ran to the bathroom screaming. The lieutenant, who had been drinking quite heavily at the party, apologized and drove himself home despite pleas from his fellow officers to let one of them drive him.

The lieutenant, a 12-year veteran of the force, was indicted by a grand jury for animate object penetration, a felony sex crime. He later pleaded guilty to misdemeanor assault and battery, claiming he was drunk and that he didn't know what he was doing. And as for driving home in his police squad car while so completely intoxicated, the prosecuting attorneys could not charge him with anything there because no blood-alcohol test was administered at the time. And just because he claims he was filthy drunk, any half-ass attorney could easily argue that how could he know if he was drunk if he was drunk, therefore his claim of drunkenness can't be taken as coherent fact, only in this instance of course.

Yes, that is the way it goes. He was given a break because he was a cop. No doubt a white cop. Fair is a relative term when it comes to the law.

And then there is the case in Miami where an FBI agent was driving his car down the wrong side of a highway while intoxicated and collided head on with an oncoming car that was carrying two young black men, brothers. The brothers were killed instantly while the FBI agent survived with minor injuries. Policemen arriving on the scene concluded that the young black men were driving on the wrong side of the road and caused the accident. No objection from the young men who lay dead. Police sent the FBI agent to the hospital without even testing him for blood-alcohol.

It doesn't have to be this way. Fair is fair and unfair is unfair. Be kind to your neighbor. Speak to your fellow employee. Walk up to him or her and introduce yourself. Smile when they pass by, or at least nod if you don't have an easy smile. We are all out here together and it is time we accept it...

...ACCEPT IT

It is still so hard for me to accept that there is emptiness in this family that cannot be filled. I see, or sense, this emptiness in my youngest boy as he enters puberty. He is at the age where he is interacting with girls and I can't help but wonder what he thinks and feels towards the opposite sex. He has never had a mother. He has never known the love or affection of a nurturing presence. Of course there has always been my mom, his grandmother, to give him that special maternal warmth that only a woman can give, but she only has him for a brief period once or twice during the year, and then she is but a voice in the phone or an email for the rest. He was always a quiet child (a blessing of sorts), but sometimes I sense a withdrawal in him, and any attempt I make at dialogue with him is rarely enlightening.

And sometimes I sense anger. In times past whenever the mention of his mother would come up in passing, he would never have much to say. But now he quickly, and sharply, points out that he doesn't have a mother— end of conversation. I wish I could believe that, in time, it won't matter to him, but I see the way it effects my oldest boy who is a man now and I know that it will never get better.

Oh sure, he will be able to carry on and life a happy, prosperous life if he so chooses, but there will always be the empty spot inside his heart where his mother used to be. And always the question why.

Why did his mother walk away and never look back? This is the question that eats at him and at me and at my oldest son. Why? I know it still eats at my oldest son even at his matured age. I know it is there because he calls me tonight to tell me that he needs to see a shrink because he can't stop chewing his hands. That's right. He wants to see a psychiatrist because he can't stop chewing his hands.

I tell you that this upset me immensely. Not the fact that he is chewing his hands. Lots of people chew their hands. I used to chew my hands. My dad used to chew his tongue. Almost everybody has chewed their fingernails at one time or another in their life. But to think that you need to see a doctor because of it alarms me. I did all I could to assure him that it is only natural and not to make a big deal of it, but he insisted that there is something wrong with him and he needs to get help. He proceeded to tell me about the large bug that he had beheaded outside of his apartment. He said it was a large bug that he didn't just step on, he said he slowly and deliberately cut off its head. I told him that everyone mutilates a bug or two in their lifetime (I didn't tell him how I used to burn the heads off of grasshoppers with my magnifying glass), but he disagreed and said that he is not a kid but an adult and shouldn't be doing something like that at his age. I told him to go see the psychiatrist at the school and hung up the phone.

Is he seeking attention? Is he perhaps reverting back to a childhood that he never really had because of being forced to grow up fast and be strong for his father who was a wreck after the breakup of our family? I don't know. But I can't help but feel that the boy is just not at peace with himself because of being rejected by the mother who brought him into this world. He just didn't understand that it wasn't his mother it was the crack cocaine.

I fear there will be no filling of this hole in their hearts. And no peace...

…PEACE

I wonder sometimes if I will ever find peace myself. It has been one thing having to deal with losing the love of my life; time is helping somewhat with this albeit ever so slowly. But nothing not even time can wash away the stigma of 'child molester'.

In Texas, J. Clifford Baxter, former Vice-Chairman of one of the largest, most powerful, companies in America, a Giant Silver Subterfuge known as Enron, apparently committed suicide near his Houston suburb home leaving behind his wife and children to grieve over the loss of a husband and a daddy. The shame of bilking millions of dollars from his fellow employees was too much for him to bear.

A cohort of Baxter's said he talked to him the week before his death about the public's reaction to Enron's fall. "They are calling us child molesters," the cohort recalled him as saying. "That will never wash off."

He could not have known how close to the truth he was. He killed himself over the shame of having stolen money from others. I suppose that if he did in fact commit suicide he had reasoned it was the only appropriate justice that could be administered, and he had to be the one to administer it. But to liken his grandest of larceny to being a child molester pretty much says it all, doesn't it? Apparently, in his view a child molester is not fit to live.

I feel sorry for his widow and the two children he left behind. The loss of a loved one is never easy. But I have no time to dwell on their misery because I deal with my own misery, a misery that I just can't ever shake, or wash off.

Things have gotten better for me now, no doubt. But I still live with the fear every day that I will be let go from my job, or talked about by someone behind my back. Of course I don't dwell on it. Of course I don't cower in fear of being found out. But every time my boss comes to me and says he needs to see me, or every time I see two people looking at me and talking between themselves, I can't help but feel for just a quick moment that dread that I have been discovered. I live with it daily; it has become a part of me. I cannot wash it off.

And I can't just pretend it is not there. If only it were that easy...

...EASY

It is amazing how it is so easy for Americans to just 'go with the flow' and never question where or why or how. We are like a nation of zombies. This is why the corporate CEOs have been so successful at controlling working American's wages. Employers get more and more every day and do so in plain sight of the workers. Workers will do nothing about it because they have become sheep. Ask them about it, and they will tell you that the CEO deserves all their money because they provide sheep with jobs and work. These sheep do not even consider striking out on their own to make money. They know nothing of the ways of the early settlers in America who had to invent ways to prosper. The sheep of today are content to follow the leader wherever he may lead them. Is there little wonder that the working American grows poorer year by year while the unscrupulous CEO gets richer?

And how does this nation of sheep carry on from day to day without any venturing forth and original thoughts of their own? Why with the help of King Medical of course, the number one industry in the United States. The medical industry has taken over where King Tobacco left off. Wall Street and the Insurance industry are all banking heavily on King Medical, and with the country being held captive by the American Medical Industry it seems a safe bet.

And how is it that the American Medical Conglomerate has captured the American public and turned them into passive sheep you ask? Why, it is because of the Magic Pill of course.

The American Medical Consortium has created a pill for every possible ailment under the sun. The American Medical Sucking Machine will never tell you that to stay healthy you must exercise. The gluttonous pigs who control the Medical American King Pharma Association do not wish for you to know that shaking you stomach around via running or swimming or any sort of exercise will do more for you than any combination of pills or synthetics could ever do. They do not wish for you to know because they want to sell you a pill -- a Magic Pill.

There are today pills for pain, pills for weight, pills for mood and pills for energy. If you have a headache, take an aspirin. If the headache is between your eyes then take a sinus pill, if it is in the back of your head then take a migraine pill.

If you are overweight, take a pill. If you want to stop eating take some legalized acid. If you want to eat all you want but pass it through take a laxative. Heaven forbid you should get out and move your fat ass around some. Heaven forbid you should discover exercise. Just take a pill to keep yourself in shape. Your pharmacist and his boss depend on it.

If you don't like the way your hair looks, take a pill to make it grow faster.

If you don't like the way you think, take a pill to speed up your brain and make you smarter.

If you don't like your sex life, take a pill. Now in chewable, one-a-day dose.

If you want to be more confident, simply take a One-a-Day Confident.

If you want to be more handsome, simply take a One-a-Day Handsome.

If you want to feel better about yourself, simply take a One-a-Day I Feel Good.

Yes, if you are depressed, don't make yourself get out and move around, just take a pill. If you are depressed about your weight, take a pill for your weight and take a pill to stop thinking about it. And if you should happen to get a headache because you are depressed about your weight, no problem, just go see your doctor because he is sure to have something for you. But whatever you do don't hurry because God forbid you should work up a sweat. The American Medical Behemoth couldn't stand that.

Consequently, people with money in America have become passive sheep, passive drugged sheep. These people have the money and the power to make significant changes in America, but instead they sit back and allow Wall Street to take their money and in return they get their One-a-Day Happy.

Thus, the CEO gets richer because he takes everything he or she can get his or her hands on while passive sheep mill about. Gluttony becomes passe as the rich CEO surrounds himself with other gluttonous pigs. They gravitate towards fenced-in neighborhoods and exclusive country clubs to separate them from the sheep they exploit. Life becomes a race to see who can be the biggest pig for the year. Asses grow wide and heavy, movement becomes restricted, jaws double and triple fold, and the white man's value increases. He can barely wipe his own ass anymore but he is a valuable commodity because he can think. Do you think I'm just being foolish?...

...FOOLISH

It is all so very obvious, foolish Earthlings. Affirmative Action is crucial to the survival of your human white race.

You humans consist of mental and physical powers. The blacks of your world possess superior physical powers. The mental potential is there, however their physical attributes are so strong that the need to rely on mental power is secondary.

In contrast, the whites of your world possess stronger mental powers. Inferior physical attributes require whites to rely heavily on brain power to survive. Lying, deceit, and trickery are tools that the whites of your world have mastered. The physical potential is there, however the white's mental prowess has become so dominant that, via the development and implementation of synthetic power, ie weaponry and machinery, the need for physical power is no longer important.

As your Earth enters a new time millenium your Earth America society must continue to take steps to balance out its physical and mental attributes or else the black human race will be exterminated while at the same time the white human race will evolve into brains sitting inside hunks of sweaty, rolling flesh with useless, inadequate extremities.

The white male intellect's practice of the phasing out and replacing his sexual organ with a strap-on phone/fax combo kit is testimony to this.

Without Affirmative Action the white man will become more physically inadequate and consequently reliant on synthetic aids to survive until the very oxygen he breaths becomes a poison to his over-sensitized body.

Tim Wise, of Speak Out, was on the Virginia Tech campus last week. Mr. Wise is one of America's leading anti-racist activists as well as being one of the most popular speakers on its campuses today. His book "Little White Lies: The Truth About Affirmative Action and Reverse Discrimination" is currently being used by numerous colleges around the country to study institutionalized racism and its effects in America.

Affirmative Action has drawn criticism as of late by a group of white people who claim that it is a form of reverse discrimination. (For those of you who don't understand what reverse discrimination is, reverse discrimination is simply a fancy word for discrimination but with an adjective in front to bring more attention to the fact that an injustice is being perpetrated on poor innocent white folk.) A group white parents have gotten together and complained that, simply because their little Dick or little Jane didn't get admitted into the college of their choice, it must be the fault of Affirmative Action and therefore Affirmative Action must go.

Hence, the birth of Proposition 209. Proposition 209 (and I quote) "prohibits the state, local governments, districts, public universities, colleges, and schools, and other government instrumentalities from discriminating against or giving preferential treatment to any individual or group in public employment, public education, or public contracting on the basis of race, sex, color, ethnicity, or national origin." In other words, Proposition 209 states that it doesn't matter whether you're black or brown or yellow or blue the white guy's got the green so 'he da man.'

Mr. Wise did an excellent job of pointing out how the attack on Affirmative Action's preferential treatment rendered towards blacks is being levied by white people who are the recipients of preferential treatment on a daily basis in America. The preferential treatment afforded white people today include preferred status admittance into certain organizations (or country clubs) around the country, preferred status employment opportunities at most companies around the U.S. where whites comprise 97% of all upper-management positions, preferred status for relocating into new neighborhoods, preferred status on consumer loans for automobiles and homes, preferred status for credit cards, and the list goes on and on.

Wise had many valid points. However, I felt that there was one major point that he failed to bring up -- the fact that the *very survival* of the white race as we know it depends on Affirmative Action. Here's why.

The white race depends on Affirmative Action because for every one black person admitted into a college or university in the U.S., there will one white person in America who will be forced to actually have to learn how to work. This is all good for whites, because as the white intellectual collegiate hones his brain into the sharpest of tools, his ability to use his body to actually apply his sharp theories becomes an ever-increasing obstacle. The white intellect of today has become so emulsified with bookish technical data of microscopic computations and formulations that it seems he has no capacity remaining to understand and implement the everyday menial tasks that require practical application, physical labor, and common sense.

For instance, the white intellectual engineer of today can design a revolutionary compound that will double the life of every automobile tire in America, yet ask him to change a tire and he will be lost.

The modern day white intellectual technician can tell you, to the 1/1000th decimal place, the number of calories in each and every morsel on your plate, yet ask them to cook and they will stare at you dumbfounded.

As the white intellectual continues to distance himself from any task requiring some measure of physical exertion he becomes unbalanced. His stress rises and his overall health declines as he becomes addicted to a sedentary pursuit of mental masturbation. The ever increasing need for mental health therapy and all manner of medications are a testament to this.

If you think I'm crazy, just look at white societies' most profound inventions over the past century-- the automobile, the television, and the computer. The one thing that they all have in common is they can each be operated while squarely planted upon one's ass. If white America had to use a computer while running in place would it be as popular of a device? I doubt it.

We need Affirmative Action so that whites can develop the skills necessary for the applications of survival. Blacks already have these skills, forced to learn them by an enslaving white society. America needs Affirmative Action so that blacks can help to teach these skills of survival to an ignorant white America.

Everyday, the white intellectual Road Scholar of today runs the risk of suffocating in an enclosed automobile on a hot day because he doesn't know how to operate the hand crank of a non-electric window.

Take heed America. The white intellect is in danger of extinction. Oh the misery...

...A CHILD'S MISERY

See that oldest son of mine, he grows so tall and strong,
at the age now to question, what is right and what is wrong.
He comes to me, his dad, and I do my very best,
to give him all my wisdom, and put his mind to rest.
He'd like to ask his mom sometimes, but he can't for you see,
she's high on crack and on her back, over in Pulaski.

He just became a teenager, a special day it was,
but he didn't seem too happy, explained "It's just because."
We had some cake and ice-cream, and all his friends were there,
but not his mom, no word from her, didn't see her anywhere.
She could not be there, would not you see,
she's high on crack and on her back, over in Pulaski.

And see that youngest son of mine, so handsome and so lean,
so full of playground energy, it's hard to keep him clean.
Will he be a doctor, or president? These things I cannot know,
I just do my best to keep him fed, the fuel that makes him grow.
And does his mom do anything? She can't, she won't, for you see,
she's high on crack and on her back, over in Pulaski.

When days are tough, they are my strength, these loving boys of mine,
I thank the Lord for blessing me with sons that are so fine.
I try to keep them happy, don't talk about the past,
"Be children, grow slowly, for the world will take you fast.

Love your neighbor as yourself, and do not lie, cheat, or steal,
And say a prayer for your poor mom, her sickness God to heal."

Perhaps one day she'll hear those prayers, though grown
men they may be,
God willing he will help her, and clear her mind to see.
That while they've grown, all on their own,
their hearts were never free,
from the pain of loving their only mom...
a child's misery...

...THANKSGIVING

It is Thanksgiving Day and I am feeling like a million bucks. I am home alone but that is a good thing on this holiday because the boys are at their grandparent's house. Jarian called this morning and said his grandfather had called him and asked him to come down to visit, and Jarian said he would come see them and bring Landon along. I was elated to hear this because when I spoke to him last he had not been planning to go. He said he did not want to be around all his aunts and uncles because he would feel uncomfortable. I admit that I can relate. When I would visit relatives who I had not seen in a long, long while, and some I had never met, I would feel out of place as well. But only for a while, and then nature kicked in and I would always feel happy to be around relatives. Even if we didn't have lots in common, it was something comfortable about them.

And this is what I want for my boys. And this is what I believe can be if they just allow it to happen. There is even a possibility they might even see their mom. And I have sat here alone, although I am not truly alone because Jarian's dog is visiting our dog, and there is a beautiful dish in my kitchen at this very moment, and although she is not preparing me a meal, she is a meal because I am speaking of that beautiful roasted turkey sitting in my oven making my apartment smell so damn good. I make myself step outside for a minute so that I can walk back in and take in the full aroma of that gorgeous dish that I am going to eat here shortly.

So perhaps things will get better. I have high hopes. Maybe everything's coming up roses.

Speaking of roses, I just got a job delivering flowers. After two weeks of more rejection letters from companies, I was offered a job at a local florist to do deliveries. I had applied a few weeks back. It was the first application I had ever filled out that did not ask about my criminal record. It did ask about my driving record and that is flawless knock on wood.

So I need to stop worrying, at least I have a job for now. I will give myself a stroke if I don't stop this fretting...

...FRETTING

I go for an interview today and I am fretting. It is the first really good possibility for a *real* job making *real* money and I am so nervous. This company called me last week and the woman who called said that one of her computer programmers had given her my application to check out because he felt I would be good for an assistant managers position the company had open. I had evidently applied for a computer programmer position but wasn't qualified enough for that but it seems they still like my qualifications and want me to come down as soon as possible for an interview. I am going this afternoon.

But I am fretting. Big time.

Am I fretting because I am nervous about the interview? Not at all. Am I fretting over whether or not I will know enough to get the job? Not at all. I have confidence in my abilities. I know computers. No, I'm fretting because I know they will ask me whether or not I have a criminal record and I will be faced with the same old dilemma that I keep having to deal with every time - whether to say "yes, I have a criminal record and thank you for your time, good day now," or whether to say "no, no criminal record, and by the way did I mention I have children at home to feed?"

It just doesn't seem fair. Why do I have to keep dealing with this over and over? It's killing me. Did the Commonwealth's Attorney know that he was dealing me a death blow when he did this to me? Of course he did. He knew that he was branding me, crippling me-for life. He wanted to do it. He wanted to punish me for being a fool, for being a traitor to my race, he wanted to teach this 'nigger loving SOB' a lesson, and of course, he wanted the victory.

He wanted to win the case. That's what it's all about in his profession, winning cases. And the niggers were always easy targets and easy wins for him, but taking this nigger lover down would be oh so sweet. Oh the dehumanization...

...DEHUMANIZATION

I once saw the infamous Jewish attorney Alan Dershowitz on the "Geraldo Live" show condemning the "hate radio" of the Rush Limbaugh's and Jerry Falwell's and Pat Buchanan's in the media. Dershowitz was claiming their brand of rhetoric "dehumanized" Black and Jewish people everywhere. Though I agree with Dershowitz about Falwell & Buchanan because they are two of the biggest bigots in the public arena, I wonder if the extremely affluent Dershowitz ever noticed that the American economy itself "dehumanizes" black people on a constant basis. I wonder if Dershowitz, as he cruises through the streets of New York reading his newspaper in the back seat of his stretch limousine, ever notices the conditions of the neighborhoods that inner city blacks find themselves trapped in. I wonder if he ever thinks for a second that life in drug-infested squalor known as the 'projects' in America is a little "dehumanizing" to all those trapped there. I just wonder.

The wealthy are always getting on TV to talk about what they are doing to help the poor and underprivileged, but it never stops them from using every last loophole they can to keep from having to pay their fair share of taxes. The wealthy always believe that they deserve every last penny they get, whether it is one million or one billion, and they never want to sacrifice any of it in order to make this world a better place. Whether the money came from a rich inheritance or whether a stock market investment paid off, the rich believe that the money was hard earned. Things will never get better unless the extremely wealthy and powerful are willing to make sacrifices of their own, or are made to make sacrifices. But they will never be made to make sacrifices because that would involve enforcement and the rich and powerful own the law and manipulate the law in America.

The rich would have you believe that they are donating money to help a cause, but they wouldn't give a dime to anyone if it weren't for the fact that they get a nice tax break from Uncle Sam for giving the money. If the rich really wanted to help the poor they would pay the working poor better wages. Better wages would put more people to work. However, the rich wouldn't dream of giving up anything. They feel that all money should flow through their hands first so that they can dole it out to where it needs to go because, of course, the rich know best. Only the rich can ascertain what is a worthy cause and what is not. The rich feel they should be the ones to decide where, and to whom, all monies should go to. Consequently, the wealthy white man remains in power.

And now the white man wants to do away with Affirmative Action while at the same time using his influence and clout to have his way. The greedy white man is clueless to the damage he is causing the country and the world. He has become a self-centered, egotistical monster, the most dangerous social predator known to man since the days of the Tyrannosaurus Rex.

You may think I am crazy because slavery was ended over a hundred years ago, but I tell you the residue still stains American society. In my day, the infamous heavyweight champion of the world, Mohammad Ali, visited a sports club in NY City and was the first black ever allowed to step foot through the doors of the hallowed 'white man's club,' except for the custodian and bathroom attendant of course. And today, golfing sensation Tiger Woods is playing golf on courses that have never before allowed blacks to play on. Yet, whites still swear that prejudice is a thing of the past. It is the typical white response. Whites learned long ago how to turn a deaf ear to the suffering of blacks, and how to bury their head in the sand so as not to see the strange fruit hangin from the poplar trees.

And the white man and his offspring cry foul when they can't get into the college they want to because Affirmative Action has given hope and opportunity to a black child instead. These white brothers and sisters of mine make me ashamed to be a part of the white race. They are so clueless and self-centered that they make me want to puke. They must be crazy...

...CRAZY

And I think sometimes that I must have been crazy for ever letting things go as far as they did. No, not with the young girl -- I feel I was very stupid and gullible for letting that happen, but not crazy. I mean after the fact, after my night with the young girl, I must have been out of my head for letting the law railroad me the way it did.

Four days after the night in question I was at work when I received a phone call from a police detective wanting me to come down to the station to talk with him. He wouldn't tell me what it was about over the phone. I assumed he wanted to talk to me about my estranged wife who was running around with a gang of crackheads. I had heard rumors that she and her young boyfriend had been dealing the drug as well. I naturally assumed the detective wanted to talk to me about that.

I met the detective in at the station. He led me into a small room, empty save for a little table and two chairs. It was obvious to me that it was some sort of interrogation room. We sat down at the table and the first thing he asked me was did I know a girl named April. I was totally caught off guard. Perplexed, I replied that I did.

His next question was did I know she was only thirteen years old. I almost fell out of the chair. I felt my heart, my shoulders, my whole being sink. I couldn't believe it. I told him that no, I didn't know.

He then opened up a folder that he had placed on the table and he began asking me all these questions, questions like was she in my apartment on the night in question, did I touch her breasts, did she touch me back, did I do this and did she do that. I was in a mild state of shock at this point and the questions all became blurred and seemed to run together.

I told him that yes, she was over at my place the other night, but no, I did not touch her, no, she did not touch me, no...no...no. I denied everything at first.

He asked me why would the girl claim that I did, and I said I don't know why. After a few more questions and denials on my part, the detective got up out of his chair and said that he would need a statement from me. He said I had the choice of giving a statement on tape or of giving him a written statement. I opted for the written statement.

The detective gave me a steno pad and a pen and asked me to give him a statement of what happened or didn't happen that night then he left the room and left me alone to my thoughts.

My head was spinning at this point. My whole body felt so heavy and my heart was crushed. I couldn't believe the cruel twist my life had taken again. There I was feeling so good about having met this beautiful young lady whom I thought was a Godsend to me, and here I find she was just a child who had lied to me about her age and no doubt everything else she told me. And not only was I devastated that she was not the answer to my prayers, I was now facing a criminal charge. I was absolutely crushed. There I had been grieving over the loss of my wife for months upon months and now I was dealt another blow that was equally as demoralizing. I just couldn't take it. I gave up.

I sat there for a long moment staring at that blank sheet of paper and then I wrote:

Whatever April said happened did happen. I was wrong.

I can't recall now if I put anything in there about not knowing her true age or not. I would hope that I had, but I guess it really didn't matter to me at that point. What could I have said? I signed the paper. I buried myself right there without even knowing it and without even caring. I just didn't care. I was beaten. I had no fight left, no desire to even try.

First, I had lost my wife. She was the love of my life, the one I had committed to. I had wanted to spend the rest of my life with her, to grow old with her. I used to envision her and I sitting on our porch in our old age in rocking chairs reflecting back on what a challenge it had been raising our mixed children and savoring our accomplishment. I suppose every couple with children wonders sometimes what life will be like after the children are raised and gone. But Carolyn was not only the love of my life she and my family were my very reason for existing. I felt that I was doing God's will by mixing races and being one people in his universe. But it had all fallen apart, horribly, and then along comes this other lovely princess who I feel attracted to and who makes me forget my pain when I am simply near her or talking to her, and it suddenly just turned to shit too and I could not believe it all. Nothing like being kicked in the gut while you are down. I didn't want to go on.

I called the detective back into the room and handed him the statement. He took it and looked at it and told me to wait there. He came back a moment later accompanied by another detective and they handcuffed me and walked me out to a cruiser and took me to the county jail where I was processed and locked up.

Yes, I guess at that point I was out of my head. Mad. I never even saw the police report myself, yet I signed a paper stating that whatever was in it was the truth. I don't know what I was thinking, but of course I wasn't thinking. I just didn't care.

And then I went and waived my right to an attorney and it seemed I did everything I could to bury myself. I wasn't being rational, but after the initial shock of the arrest wore off I did try to fight. I was totally cognizant when I waived my right to a court appointed attorney. I didn't like lawyers and I didn't want to hide behind one of those scumbags. I had a mouth and I could defend myself. That, in my opinion, was the way it should be.

Looking back, perhaps I wasn't thinking rationally. But I think I was. I knew I was innocent, innocent to a degree because I was also guilty to a degree, but I certainly didn't molest this girl and I never dreamed at that point that I could be convicted, much less go to jail, for what had taken place that night.

Looking back, I really dug myself a deep hole over what happened...

...HAPPENED

That night is when it happened.

When I arrived home she was waiting up for me. The kids staying over for my son's sleepover were in his room asleep or else playing on his Atari. April's cousin was asleep on my bed back in my room.

After I sat down on the couch beside her April told me that her mother said she could spend the night. I was surprised by this, but elated as well. I didn't question it because I just figured her mother was letting her stay here because her brother was here too and she would help watch him. After all she was a senior in high school – or so I thought. It was after midnight at this point. We sat there and though the television was on neither one of us paid any attention to it because we were just looking at each other and talking.

We kissed for a while and held each other close and did some what amounted to petting. I wanted her badly, I was aching for her, but at the same time I didn't want to force things. I was a bit uncomfortable with her being so much younger than me and thus I didn't want to rush her or myself for that matter. I felt that we would have plenty of time to get to know each other better if it was meant to be.

After a while of kissing and embracing she pulled away from me and got up and went on into the back to go to bed with her cousin. I had a blanket I kept on the couch and I laid it down on the floor and lay down to try to get some sleep when the next thing I knew there was April again standing there above me. She lay down beside me and we were at it again, kissing and groping each other. But only for a few brief minutes this time because I was the one who pulled away from her this time and I told her that this was not the right thing to do and asked her to please go to the back and go to bed.

After she had gone I lay there for a while with my mind racing. I hoped she would come back up front again and lay down beside me while at the same time I was hoping she wouldn't. I kept telling myself to just take it slow there would be another time don't rush things and mess them up.

I didn't see her anymore that night and finally dozed off and the next morning I got up and fixed everyone breakfast and April and I chatted for a while and then she and her cousin left. She called me that night and we talked some more. We talked about her moving in with me after she graduated from school in the summer. It all seemed so perfect to me. I asked her again like I had a few times already if she was sure she wanted to be with me because I was much older than her. She said that she liked me and that she was sure she wanted to move in with me. Our conversation ended with some sweet words exchanged and I hung up the phone feeling like a king. It suddenly dawned on me that I hadn't thought much about Carolyn at all that whole day because my thoughts were so consumed with April and it felt good, real good, to know that perhaps I was on my way to moving on with life.

Four days later I was arrested and locked up...

...LOCKED UP

So there I was locked up again but this time for contempt of court and my mind was spinning. I was trapped.

I wanted to hold out and stand up for my rights, I wanted to be strong and take whatever they threw at me because I believed in truth and justice and that I would be proven innocent. But I was now locked up behind bars and set to remain there until my trial which could be weeks away, and there were two young boys back at home who depended on me to show up every evening to cook and to see after them and to make sure they were safe and warm. I wanted to hold out and spit in the face of the law, but they had the power, they had control, and they could care less about my two interracial boys who would wonder where their dad was when he didn't come home.

So who was going to take care of my children while I was in jail? All my relatives lived hours away and it would not be possible for them to take the children. No doubt they would be handed over to their mother who was living with her young crack dealing boyfriend in an apartment filled with drugs and guns, constant visitors in and out all day long, and God knows what else. Not the place for my boys at all. Suppose I sat in jail for weeks? One week, even one day, one second could be disastrous if my estranged wife was to take the children to stay with her.

I could take the plea deal the Commonwealth's Attorney had offered up at one point which was to plead guilty and be given a five-year suspended jail sentence and be placed on active probation for that same period of time. I would not have to go to jail but I would have to report to a probation officer every month for five years. In other words, plead guilty and stay out of jail.

I mulled it over. I didn't want to plead guilty because I knew I wasn't guilty but what choice did I have at this point? And how bad could a felony conviction really hurt me? I didn't really care if someone wanted to call me a child molester, I knew I wasn't. I didn't care if someone wanted to label me on some criminal record rap sheet somewhere that no one ever really saw. Remember this was before the days of the internet and social media and I thought that really not too many people would ever know about my conviction. And I really didn't care. I knew the truth and as long as I could live with myself, I didn't care what anyone else thought. This was between me and the Lord and he is the Supreme Judge and he knows I am innocent so what did I care if some bigoted judge wants to brand me as guilty on some piece of paper. It didn't matter. It couldn't hurt me that bad. Sticks and stones can break my bones but mere words can never hurt me. I made up my mind.

I called the jailer over and told him to send for the Commonwealth's Attorney because I wanted to deal. I signed the confession that said I was admitting my guilt and then I was led back into an empty courtroom again except for the judge and the Commonwealth's Attorney and me and the bailiff and another man who later turned out to be my probation officer. I plead guilty to the felony offense of Indecent Liberties with a Minor and the judge accepted my guilty plea and sentenced me to five years in prison, all suspended provided I met all terms of active probation for that same period of time.

Guilty. Guilty as charged. The prosecutor had done me dirty and got me. Without any trial and without so much as a whimper I was guilty.

After I was sentenced I had to go back to the jail area and give blood because all convicted felons were now required to have their DNA placed on file and once that was completed I walked out of that jail and into the fresh air and sunshine a free man but a convicted child molester.

It didn't matter to me. It didn't feel any different to be a convicted felon, and it's not like I was physically marked or branded in any way so that people I pass on the street could see I am a convicted felon so how bad can it be I thought?

If only I would have known.

EPILOGUE

The boys and I finally did make it through. We made it through by the grace of God and with the help of family and some wonderful dear friends. The boys are grown men now and are healthy and happy and good people and I praise the Lord for that. They could have gone the other way. I couldn't be more proud of them.

I wrote a lot about myself in this story. I didn't do it for sympathy because trust me I have lived a blessed life. Like the song says you can't always get what you want, but you get what you need. I wanted to show that I was/am not a monster, and how the effects of a criminal record are crippling in so many ways that people may not have ever thought about.

I deprived my boys of so much when they were growing up because of my conviction. Besides the constant financial difficulties we struggled with, I also missed out on going to and participating in so many of their high school games and events because I was too ashamed and embarrassed to go out in public. The shame in a crime involving a child has far reaching effects, as it should, but just be sure that the accused is in fact someone that preys upon children. The law and their prosecutors don't seem to care either way - all they want is their win-loss record to look good.

My ex-wife Carolyn is long gone now. The effects of a prolonged crack cocaine addiction finally got the best of her. She suffered a massive stroke about 20yrs ago that paralyzed her on one side and she couldn't walk or even talk after that. I went to see her at the nursing home she was in and when I walked into her room she was sitting propped up on pillows in her bed watching a television on the wall in front of her and when she first saw me her eyes got big with fear and I just stood there smiling at her through tear-filled eyes and I could see hers finally soften up and then her attention went back to the television. I sat down beside her and held her hand for a while and talked to her about the boys and what they were up to. She looked at me sometimes but most of the time she just watched the cartoon playing on the television and giggled. She wasn't all there anymore; her stroke had been massive. After a time I got up to leave and when she looked at me it seemed her eyes were pleading for me not to go. I squeezed her hand hard and turned away and walked out. It was all I could do to get out of there fast so that she didn't see me break down and sob uncontrollably. Her face and body were all swollen up now from atrophy and she wasn't the amazing beauty that she had once been but she still looked so very beautiful to me and I still loved her so and it just devastating to see her that way. My broken heart was just broken some more.

I stopped in again a few years later to visit with her at the nursing home and she was propped up in bed the same way watching TV. This time she didn't show any fear in her eyes when I walked into her room and she even smiled. I had a short visit with her and it was a nice visit, but once again she mostly watched TV and giggled some. That was the last time I ever saw her. She passed away a year later.

There were parts of this manuscript that made Carolyn seem like a terrible person but she was not she was an amazing beautiful woman but she fell victim to that damn crack cocaine that took over her mind and body and soul just like it did so very many good people, so many black people, for a period there in America. She was such a strong person that all along I thought one day she would beat her addiction to that damn crack cocaine and perhaps she finally even did towards the end but alas the drug and its remnants beat her in the end. Such a waste. Such an absolute waste.

It is unfortunate that the boys' memories of her are mostly bad ones from when after she had become addicted and changed, but before that Carolyn was a true super lady, wife and mother. I hate that the boys never had the chance to reconnect or bond with her as I hoped they would do one day, as I KNEW they would one day. They need to know that their mom was truly special and that they are special too. Not better, not superior, but special.

All life is special. Life is a miracle and I truly believe we all have a purpose in this world; we are all here for a reason. But Carolyn, she was special. She was black and she was beautiful and she was special.

And this is something I don't understand about society today. I see so many beautiful black people out there struggling to survive financially mainly and I also see so many white people who are financially set yet who are struggling with happiness and contentment and who go out marching against the BLM and others while spewing hatred to make themselves feel better simply because they have nothing better to do with their lives or they lack inner peace and I wish I could make them see that there is no more fulfilling, satisfying feeling then to open your heart to others who may be different from you and in doing so you will unlock happiness and fulfillment like you never knew existed. Like they say, free your mind and your ass will follow. Brother I am here to tell you that it is true. Opposites attract. It is only natural. It is time for people to come together and leave the past behind. It is time.

In closing, again, I am not looking for sympathy here, nor am I looking for the young girl to be blamed or shamed or chastised somehow. She truly was innocent. She was but a young girl doing what young girls do in seeking attention by trying to act grown and she was clueless as to possible repercussions or consequences for me for her actions. I was the adult and should have been more cautious and alas I was not. I was a gullible, believing in others type person and what can I say I still am today. I believe in giving people the benefit of the doubt - I think that's the way it should be. But alas, perhaps it's my fatal flaw.

Right now in America there is ongoing legislation by some states that would make a crime involving a child punishable by death – it unnerves me to think I could have been looking at death when I never even knew I was breaking the law. The truth is there are two sides to every story. If by sharing this I can help the next person that gets caught in the same dilemma I was in then I can feel good about sharing it. I hope I can.

Because as God is my witness, I am not a child molester.

In Memory of Carolyn L. Sherman

She was special

May God rest her soul

AUTHOR BIO

Name: T.J. Kerekes, III

Age: 68

The Author

(Yearbook Picture Va Tech, Class of '99)

My boys... young grown

...and those damn dogs

www.ingramcontent.com/pod-product-compliance
Lightning Source LLC
LaVergne TN
LVHW090404210926
848480LV00002B/438

* 9 7 9 8 8 9 2 2 8 5 5 2 0 *